Produced By:

 and 

WE MAGNIFY YOU

Discovery Collection

THIS BOOK BELONGS TO:

____

About the WE MAGNIFY YOU Discovery Collection

Families are at the core of our Kingdom Communities. The WE MAGNIFY YOU album provides us with a wonderful opportunity to develop and strengthen the expression of worship in our homes.

The We Magnify You Discovery Collection has been designed for parents, guardians, teachers and children to experience and explore the songs together. Each section in this collection helps our families to develop a deeper and stronger understanding of who God is, releasing a whole-hearted expression of worship unto Him.

For each song on the WE MAGNIFY YOU album, we have a workbook with the lyrics and specially created activities.

Enjoy taking time together to consider what the lyrics mean. Explore scripture verses that tell us more about each song. Engage in fun activities, including word puzzles and coloring games.

Through it all we can together gain a deeper understanding of how the words we sing reflect the lives we must live, as we align ourselves to God.

Now that is a beautiful thing!

Guidance for Parents

The WE MAGNIFY YOU worship album from Congress MusicFactory contains prayers and songs from Dr. Noel Woodroffe and saints from Elijah Centre and Kingdom Communities across Congress WBN.

WE MAGNIFY YOU is a powerful expression of worship and praise to our Lord. Each workbook in the We Magnify You Discovery Collection explores the lyrics of the songs, sharing explanations, key scriptures and fun activities.

These resources will help us to align our lives, our families and our communities to the words that we lift unto God.

This collection includes lyrics, lessons and activities for all **8 songs** on the WE MAGNIFY YOU worship album:

- 1 – You Alone
- 2 – Unto You
- 3 – We Magnify You
- 4 – We Glorify Your Name
- 5 – Behold the Lord
- 6 – Holy is the Lamb
- 7 – God is Here (Hallelujah)
- 8 – Amen!

Scan to download BONUS activity pages and more resources!

1

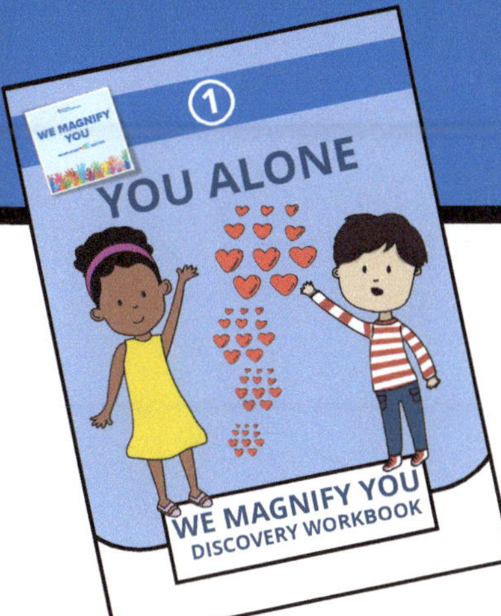

YOU ALONE

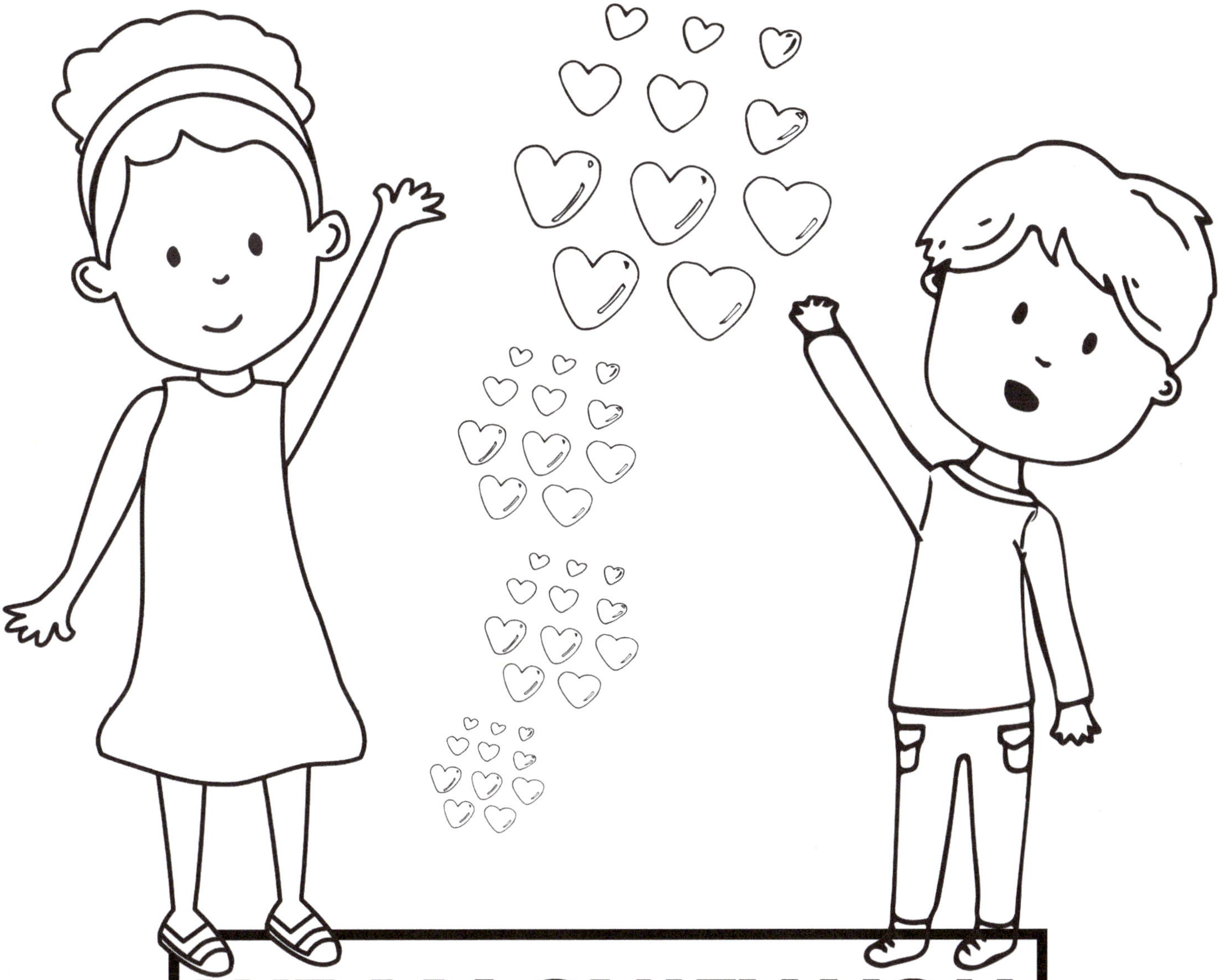

WE MAGNIFY YOU

DISCOVERY COLLECTION

How can I give all of my life to God, when there are other things I love too? I love dancing and playing outside!
Abigail
Well, maybe you should stop dancing then, because God should be the only one you love and praise!
What?!
Levi
Wait a minute... giving all of our heart to God doesn't mean we don't enjoy the life He's given us! We are worshipping God all the time, every day, in the way we live our lives. It means that we worship God like King David—with all our mind, soul and strength. That's what this song is all about.
Mr. Hebron

YOU ALONE

With all of my heart
I worship You
In all of my life
I honor You

Master of my life
I give my all
I give my praise to You alone

To You alone
You alone
I give my praise to You alone
You alone
You alone
I give my praise to You alone

You are great.
You do wonderful things.
You alone are God.
Lord my God, I will praise You
with all my heart.
I will bring glory to You forever.

Psalm 86: 10, 12

When we say the words, **"With all of my heart I worship You,"** we are saying to God, "Here is my whole heart, I give it all to You, I hold nothing back."

So when we worship, we do it with all our might, all our strength and all our heart.

When we worship, we are focusing on God, and telling Him how happy we are to have Him close to us.

Choose the correct puzzle piece to complete the heart and color it in.

Remember—we worship God with our **whole heart**!

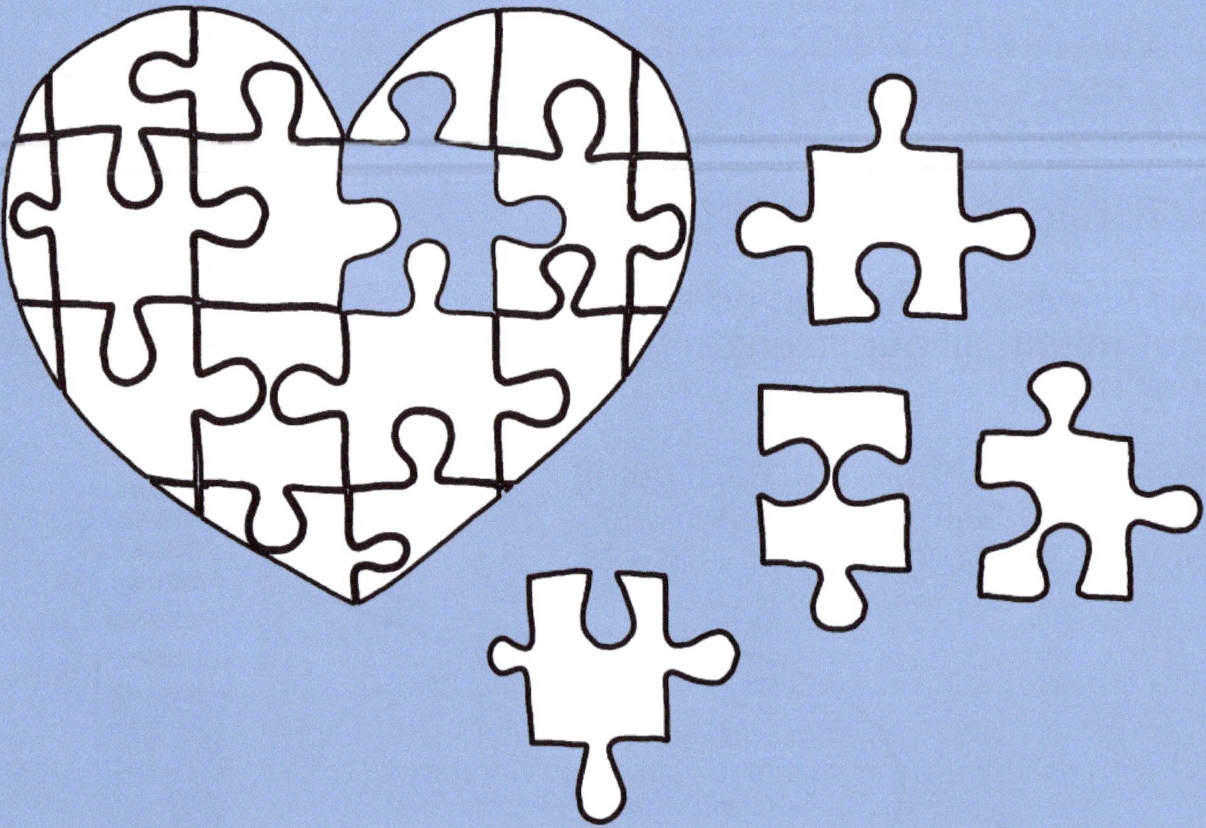

In all of my life I honor You means that whatever we are doing, we are representing God. In all our thoughts, words and actions, we are showing others exactly what He is like.

When we follow God's ways (for example, by loving others), we are honoring Him. What other kinds of behavior are honoring to God?

Let's remember that every time we sing the line, **"In all my life I honor You,"** we are transforming to become just like Him.

Activity Time
My whole heart
Help me find my way to a whole heart for God.
Psalm 9:1 I will praise You, Lord, with all my heart

Master of my life I give my all

God is the **Master of our lives**. A master is someone who is in charge of someone else.

This is the reason we give Him our all - never half-hearted.

God is our master so we must always do our very best for Him in everything that we do.

WE MAGNIFY YOU Discovery Collection: Workbook 1

Can you unscramble the following words found in the lyrics of the song?

Talk to someone about what these words mean!

HREAT	_ _ _ _ _
PROSWHI	_ _ _ _ _ _ _
OORHN	_ _ _ _ _
SRMETA	_ _ _ _ _ _
RASPEI	_ _ _ _ _ _
NALEO	_ _ _ _ _

ANSWER: HEART, WORSHIP, HONOR, MASTER, PRAISE, ALONE

WE MAGNIFY YOU Discovery Collection: Workbook 1

I give my praise to You alone

Only God deserves our praise. Praising Him means that we're telling Him that He is awesome, amazing and incredible - the best! When we give something to one person alone, it means we don't share it with anyone else.

God wants us to **give our praise to Him alone.** There may be other things in life that we value—but in worship, we are giving all our praise to our God!

Draw or write the things you love, putting them in their rightful place on the podium—under God.

God is in His right place, above everything, He is first— He is the best!

To You Alone, To You Alone

Sometimes we say something lots of times to help our brain remember it.

Think about when you have to learn new words to spell. We repeat them over and over. It's the same when we are praising God - we repeat our words of worship, so that it is written on our hearts.

To You alone God, to You alone - nothing else will get in the way of my worship to You, because I love You, Lord.

USAOENOIPTEL
YIOAYEMRGVI

ANSWER: I GIVE MY PRAISE TO YOU ALONE

WE MAGNIFY YOU Discovery Collection: Workbook 1

I give my praise to You alone

We are telling God that we praise Him alone. We thank God all the time because He is great.

When we worship God and tell Him **"I give my praise to You alone,"** we are saying that every day, on our best days and in difficult times, we will always praise Him!

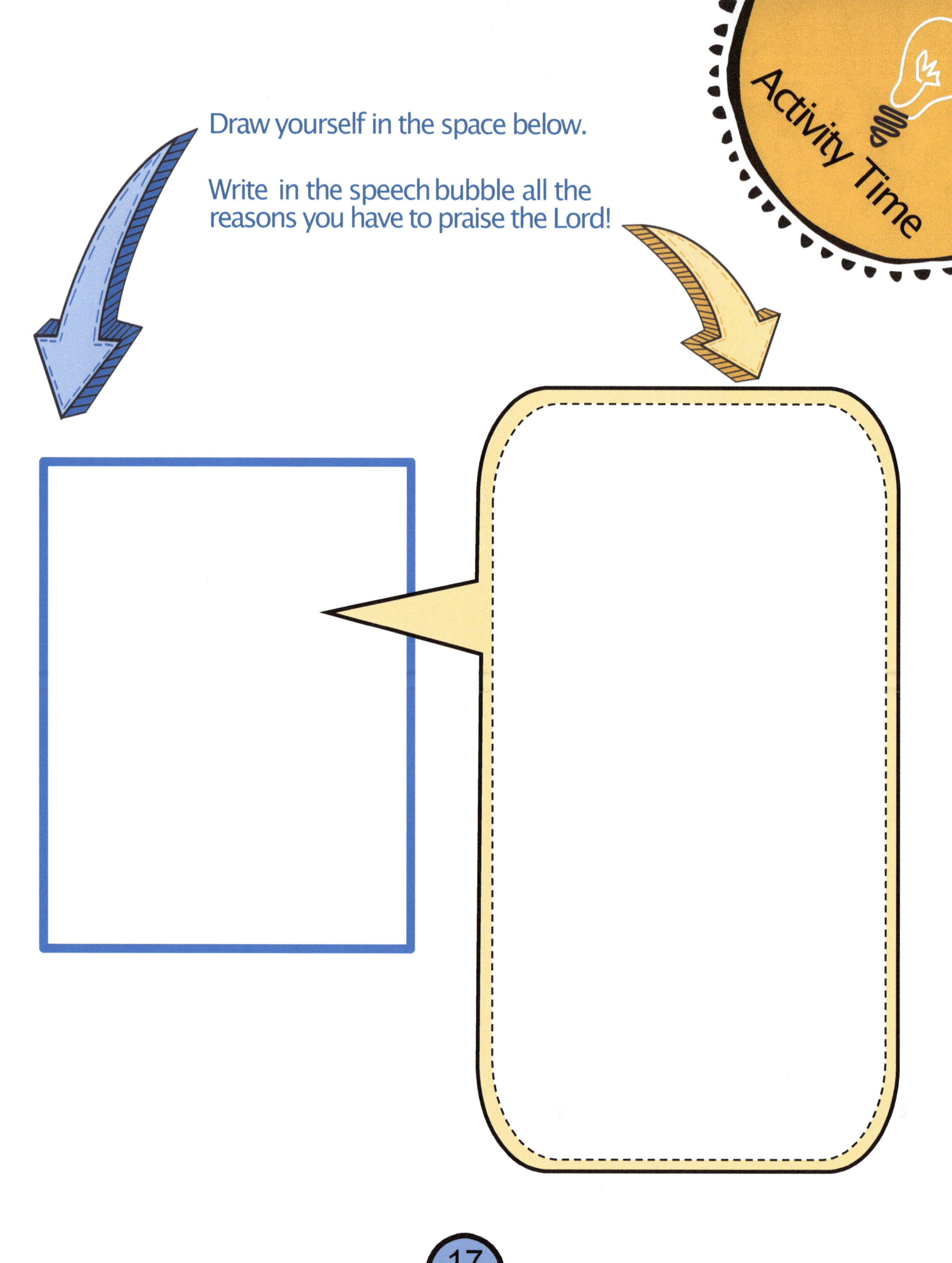

WE MAGNIFY YOU Discovery Collection: Workbook 1

We finish by telling Him once again, and we sing it loudly and joyfully so that everyone can hear the words that are coming from our hearts.

All my praise is going to You, God. No one or nothing else deserves this honor!

Look into the hearts to search for the words from the song.

Understanding these words will help you worship God.

A	S	D	E	T	Y	U	B	G	I	V	E	P	K
L	N	U	W	Q	D	T	X	O	P	C	N	I	W
L	B	S	H	D	E	G	H	R	Y	O	A	P	L
O	T	Z	L	I	F	E	S	T	O	E	G	F	C
H	E	A	N	M	A	K	H	O	U	A	L	O	E
W	O	R	T	C	H	D	A	R	E	T	S	A	M
A	L	O	P	W	O	E	R	S	A	K	P	O	V
W	L	K	E	T	Y	U	A	N	I	U	Y	R	H
M	O	R	I	E	S	I	A	R	P	L	K	U	N
W	O	S	H	Q	B	A	S	M	T	R	E	O	V
W	E	R	H	T	Y	U	I	D	L	E	P	N	P
C	V	F	E	I	U	F	D	G	O	V	A	O	K
K	L	R	D	S	P	I	O	L	P	M	I	H	U
G	I	A	L	O	N	E	V	E	H	T	F	W	E

WE MAGNIFY YOU Discovery Collection: Workbook 1

Take some time to reflect on this song. Here's some space to write down your thoughts.

MY JOURNAL

②
UNTO YOU
WE MAGNIFY YOU
DISCOVERY WORKBOOK

②

UNTO YOU

WE MAGNIFY YOU
DISCOVERY COLLECTION

Wow, Ms. Charis, you kept your arms raised in worship all the way through that song. How do you do that without getting tired?
Levi
And you're way older than us!
Why do you think we raise our hands when we worship God?
I guess it's because the song tells us to, and everybody else is doing it.
Abigail
Ms Charis
That's not wrong, but remember – God's looking at your heart. Raising your hands represents what's going on in your heart. Think about that now, as you worship God with me.

3

UNTO YOU

We lift our eyes
Unto You
We lift our hands
Unto You
We lift our voice in praise

Unto You
Unto You
Unto You
Only You
We give our worship
All of our praise
Unto You

We give our love
Unto You
We give our strength
Unto You
We give our lives in worship

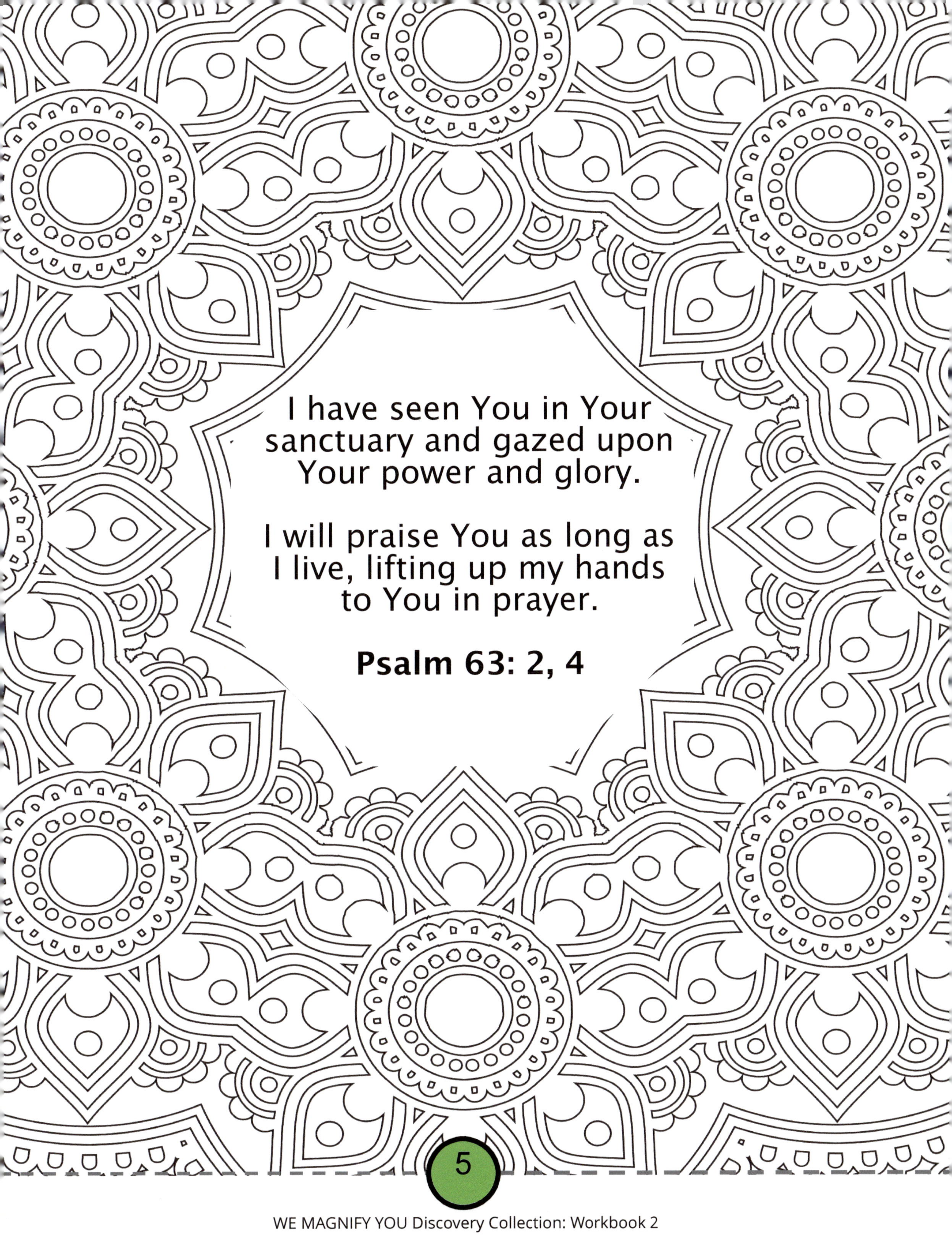
I have seen You in Your
sanctuary and gazed upon
Your power and glory.

I will praise You as long as
I live, lifting up my hands
to You in prayer.

Psalm 63: 2, 4

5

When we sing **"We lift our eyes,"** we are not talking about looking up towards the ceiling or into the sky.

Lifting our eyes means focusing on God, instead of the things around us. As we look more closely at God, we discover more about who He is and what He likes.

When we 'lift our eyes' and see God, it helps us to understand who we have to be and what He wants us to do, so that we can please Him.

WE MAGNIFY YOU Discovery Collection: Workbook 2

When **we lift our hands,** we are saying to God, "I surrender to You and give You everything. All I have is Yours."

Lifting our hands is an action we do on the outside that represents how we feel on the inside. It expresses what is in our hearts.

Psalm 63:4 reminds us that we lift up our hands when we praise God:

I will praise You as long as I live, and in Your name I will lift up my hands.

When **we lift our voice in praise,** we are telling God that He is awesome and incredible - the best!

Lifting your voice means letting everyone hear the words that are coming out of your mouth.

So when it's time for worship, raise your voice and make a joyful sound to the Lord. Let God see how excited you are about worship. Don't be shy!

Praising God with our voices together delights His heart.

Fill in the blanks with the missing words from the song.

We lift our _________
We lift our _________
We lift our _________ in praise.

WE MAGNIFY YOU Discovery Collection: Workbook 2

We give our love - we always offer to God the best of what we have.

Giving love is an action we do, no matter how we feel. We give our love to God and to others through our thoughts, words and actions.

The Bible says, in **1 Corinthians 13:4-5**:

Love is patient. Love is kind. It does not want what belongs to others. It does not brag. It is not proud. It does not dishonor other people. It does not look out for its own interests. It does not easily become angry. It does not keep track of other people's wrongs.

Inside the heart, draw or write the things we offer to God.

You could talk to someone else about this for ideas and help.

**We give God everything:
All of our love, and all that we are.**

WE MAGNIFY YOU Discovery Collection: Workbook 2

Do you remember the story of Cain and Abel? You can read about it in Genesis 4:3-7.

God was very happy with the offering Abel gave to Him, but unhappy with what Cain gave Him.

Abel gave the best of what he had **unto God.** We should always give our best to God; not just because our friends, teachers or parents tell us to, but because we want to please Him.

Use the number code to find the colors you
need to color the picture below.

What do you see?

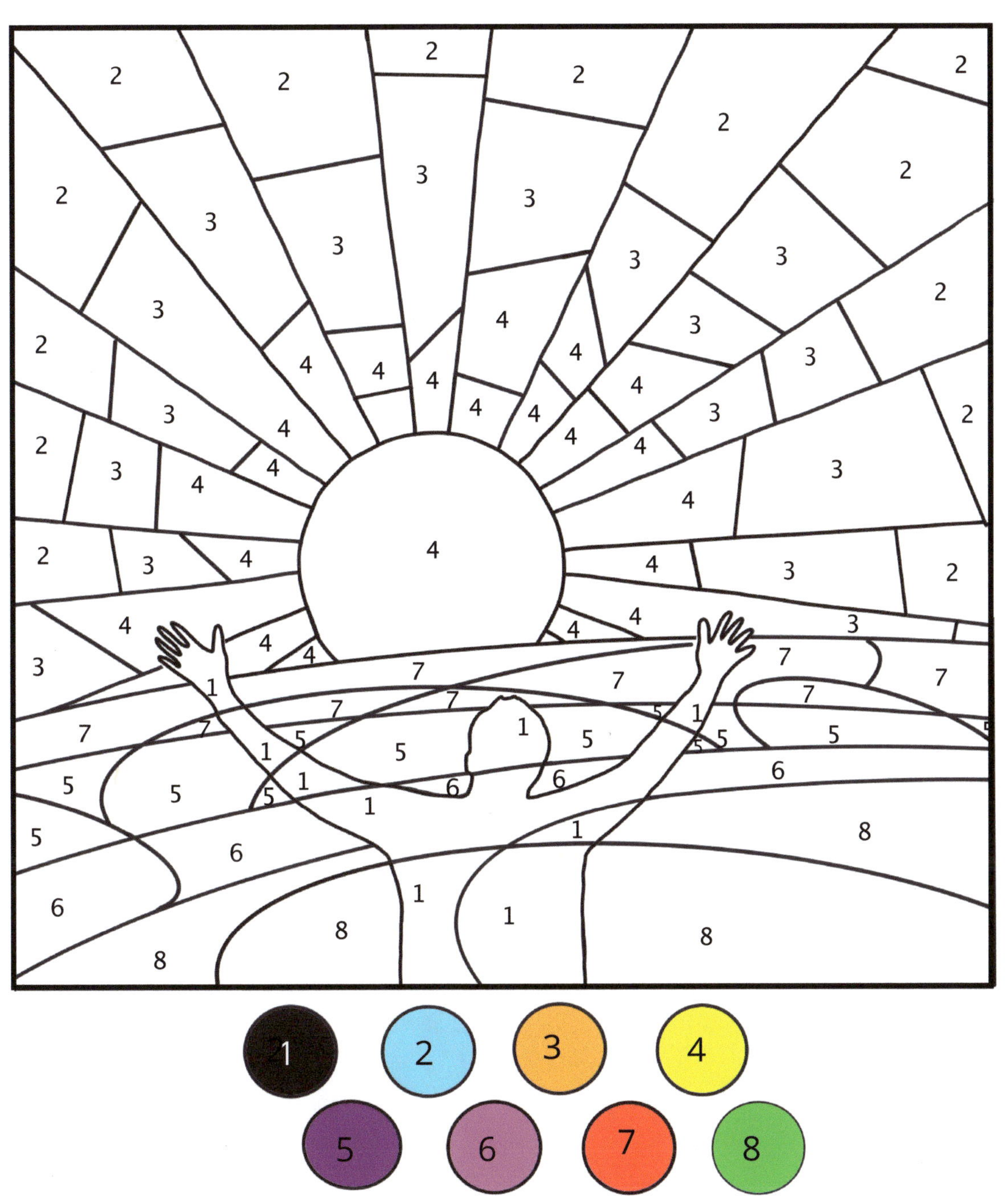

13

WE MAGNIFY YOU Discovery Collection: Workbook 2

Think about when you had to use lots of effort and energy to do something. Maybe it was running a race, lifting something or studying for a test?

We thank God for the strength He has given us, and we offer it all back to Him when we worship.

We use the strength that we have in our body, mind, soul and spirit to give God our best, as we live for Him.

Deuteronomy 6:5: *Love the Lord your God with all your heart and with all your soul. Love Him with all your strength.*

Think about what it means to give God your strength. Draw a picture of you being strong!
Activity Time

The Bible talks about praising and worshipping God your whole life. This does not mean you walk around with your hands in the air singing all day long! But it does mean praising Him as long as we are alive.

We praise Him by our lifestyle. That means doing what pleases God, even when no-one is looking. For example, when we love one another, when we're honest, and when we obey our parents and leaders - this pleases God and gives Him honor.

Unscramble the words, and then choose one of the words, and explain what it means to a friend.

<table>
<tr><td>HIPSROW
_ _ _ _ _ _ _</td><td>ADHSN
_ _ _ _ _</td></tr>
<tr><td>IRPEAS
_ _ _ _ _ _</td><td>EESY
_ _ _ _</td></tr>
<tr><td>GTRHNTES
_ _ _ _ _ _ _ _</td><td>ECIVO
_ _ _ _ _</td></tr>
</table>

ANSWER: WORSHIP, HANDS, PRAISE, EYES, STRENGTH, VOICE

WE MAGNIFY YOU Discovery Collection: Workbook 2

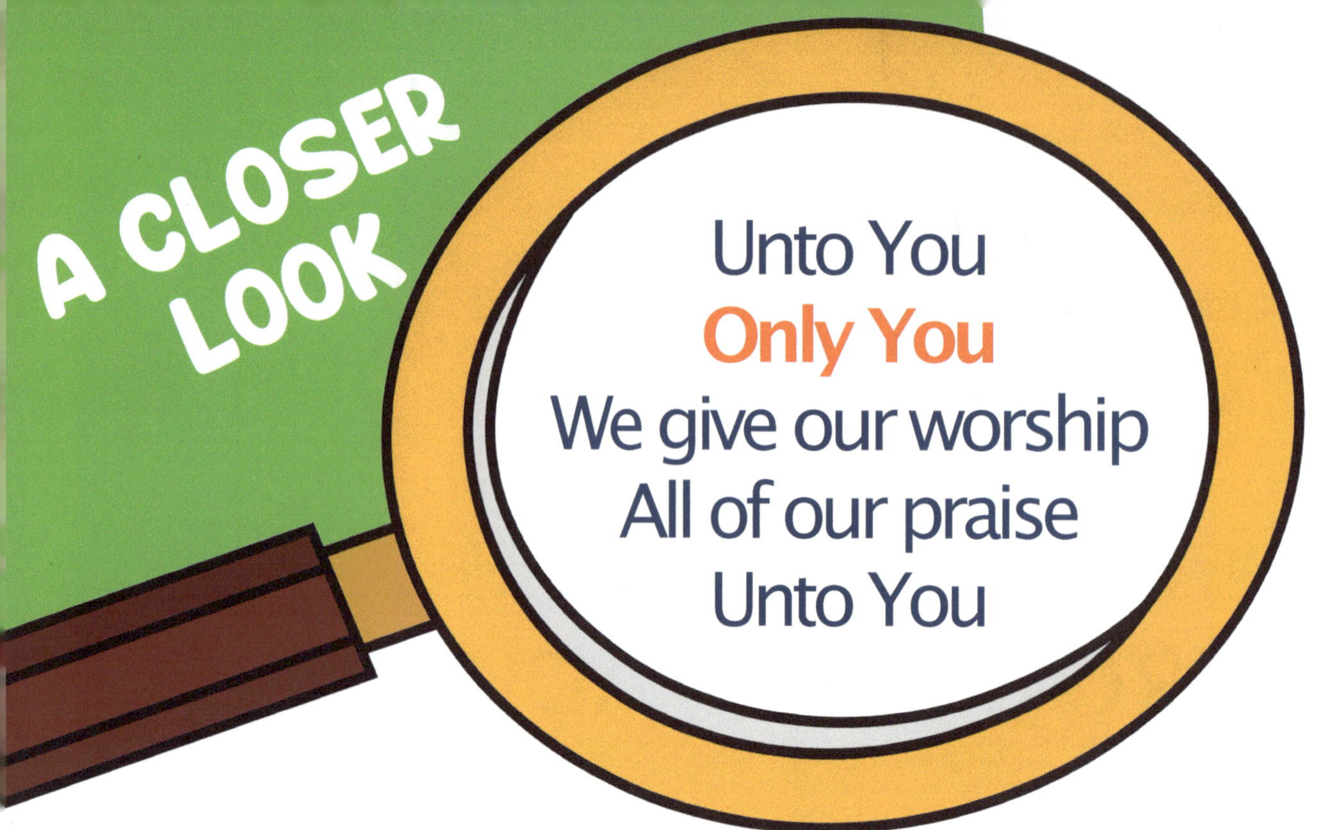

Only You means that we are willing to give up whatever we have, for God alone. These words are so simple, but very powerful.

When we say **"Only You,"** we focus all of our attention on God when it's time to pray, worship or study the Word. This means prioritizing God over other things in our lives.

We can enjoy playing with our toys and games, watching movies, playing sports or music—but these things will never have more value than the joy that comes from knowing God.

Activity Time

This song talks about giving our love in worship.

Write down some words in the hearts below that express your love for God.

Take some time to reflect on this song. Here's some space to write down your thoughts.

MY JOURNAL

③

WE MAGNIFY YOU

WE MAGNIFY YOU

DISCOVERY COLLECTION

Do I need a magnifying glass to magnify God? Isn't He already the biggest thing in the whole world?
Levi
I asked Ms. Charis about that. She told me that if I want to magnify God, I need to make Him the biggest thing in my life and in my heart.
Yes. That is true. But we also magnify Him when we live the way He wants us to. Remember when you forgave each other? You were making it easy for others to see His ways… Just like a magnifying glass!
Ms Charis
Abigail
How can you magnify God in your life?

WE MAGNIFY YOU

LYRICS

**Lord of All
Mighty God
King of Kings
There is none like You**

**Sovereign God
Righteous One
Holy Lord
There is none like You**

**We exalt Your Name
You're worthy of all praise and glory
Now as one
We lift our hands to...**

**You are faithful God
With us all along the journey
Now as one We lift our voice to....
MAGNIFY!**

**Magnify
We magnify Your Name
Lord we glorify
Glorify You**

**Magnify
We magnify Your Name
Lord we glorify
We live to give You praise**

Lord, no one is like You. You are great! You are mighty and powerful! Jeremiah 10:6

When we say, **"Lord of all, Mighty God, King of Kings,"** we are saying God is bigger than the most important person in your country, or even in the world.

If there is a president, a prime minister, or king or queen in your country, God is more important than all of them.

Saying **King of Kings** is like saying the president of all presidents, or the president's boss!

WE MAGNIFY YOU Discovery Collection: Workbook 3

There is none like You means no one is as powerful as God.

He is the Undisputed, Undefeatable, Strongest, Greatest, Mightiest, Most Awesome God of the world... and the universe!

When we say God is **Sovereign**, it means that He is in charge of everything. Nothing is out of His control!

This means that we can trust Him. Everything that happens in our lives is within His control, and His perfect plan.

WE MAGNIFY YOU Discovery Collection: Workbook 3

Righteous One means that God is holy, pure and true and is ALWAYS right.

This means we can trust Him completely to fulfill all of His promises to us. If God said it, it's true!

Holy means God is sacred, divine and very special. There is no one and nothing like God.

He is One of a kind!

Create a fingerprint animal.

Your fingerprint is completely unique –
that means no one else has a
fingerprint like yours!

WE MAGNIFY YOU Discovery Collection: Workbook 3

To **exalt** means to promote, elevate or hold in very high regard.

When we say to the Lord, **"we exalt You,"** we are telling Him that we place Him in the highest regard, above everything else that we have or love.

God is the most important thing to us.

So, by saying, **"we exalt Your name,"** we are letting Him know that we place Him first in our thoughts and in our hearts.

Draw a building in this picture that is higher than all the others.

Color in the picture, and remember that God is exalted, high above everything else!

13

To praise someone is to say good things to them and about them.

Being **worthy of all praise and glory** means that God is deserving of every compliment, every honor and every expression of adoration we can give to Him!

Because God is such a great and awesome God, we want to tell Him how important He is to us, and how much He is loved by us.

That's why when we worship, we say, "I love you, Lord! I adore you God! You are the best! You are awesome, God!"

When **we lift our hands,** we are saying to God, "I give you my whole heart. I give up everything for you."

We are surrendering to God.

To surrender to God means we let Him be in charge of our lives. Lifting our hands tells God, "I give myself to you." We often lift our hands when we worship God, showing Him that He is Lord.

To **magnify God** is to declare that God is the greatest being in the whole universe!

When we say, **"We magnify Your Name,"** we are saying to the Lord He is the biggest and best thing in our lives. He is more important than anyone or anything else!

Color in the picture, and say out loud:
"Lord, we magnify You!"

WE MAGNIFY YOU Discovery Collection: Workbook 3

Lord we glorify Glorify You

To **glorify** God is to live our lives in such a way that all our thoughts, words and actions match His ways.

When we do this, we show other people who God is through our lives.

When we glorify God, we are giving Him the biggest gift of praise we possibly can - aligning our lives to His ways.

18

Look at the words below.
Put a tick next to the ones that glorify God.

Then look at the pictures and circle the ones
that show behavior that glorifies God.

Which of these will you choose to do today?
Each choice we make can bring Him glory!

☐ Thankfulness   ☐ Joy
☐ Anger   ☐ Gentleness
☐ Patience   ☐ Jealousy
☐ Giving   ☐ Kindness
☐ Sharing   ☐ Self-control
☐ Forgiveness   ☐ Disobedience
☐ Envy   ☐ Honesty

19

Being **faithful** means always being there for someone else.

Like a very good friend, a parent, an aunt or uncle, God is always on your side and wants what's best for you.

All along the journey God has loved you, guided and watched over you. From the moment you were born until today, God has been close to you!

WE MAGNIFY YOU Discovery Collection: Workbook 3

Now as one means that we are joined together as one global community.

Together we **lift our voices** in song to magnify and glorify the Lord.

- ☐ Exalt
- ☐ Faithful
- ☐ Glorify
- ☐ Holy
- ☐ Magnify
- ☐ Praise
- ☐ Righteous
- ☐ Sovereign
- ☐ Worthy
- ☐ Journey

O	H	E	L	Y	T	F	R	I	N	A	O	H	R
L	H	S	T	R	I	I	I	W	O	R	T	H	Y
O	L	I	I	A	I	R	H	F	E	H	N	R	R
J	N	A	Y	Y	Y	G	G	L	O	R	I	F	Y
J	R	R	E	J	O	I	H	E	S	S	N	Y	N
Y	O	P	L	V	F	A	I	T	H	F	U	L	G
I	L	U	I	R	A	L	F	L	E	R	W	R	I
N	E	L	R	T	E	Y	I	G	I	O	T	N	E
R	N	O	H	N	G	R	T	A	R	O	U	I	R
T	Y	F	I	O	E	R	L	J	A	T	A	S	E
I	H	U	I	G	L	Y	A	S	I	N	L	E	V
M	A	G	N	I	F	Y	X	V	L	M	T	F	O
T	G	R	Y	R	U	I	E	O	X	P	A	N	S
I	F	G	F	R	G	O	F	L	X	S	N	T	U

Write your own words in the speech bubble below, to show how we lift up our voices in praise to God!

WE MAGNIFY YOU Discovery Collection: Workbook 3

MY JOURNAL

④

WE GLORIFY YOUR NAME

WE MAGNIFY YOU

DISCOVERY COLLECTION

When I think about God and how perfect He is, it makes me want to be more like Him. I want to do what is right all the time!
Levi
God is awesome! He is perfect and holy and so good to us. And He loves us even though we are not perfect.
Abigail
Excellent children! When you talk about God like that, you are glorifying Him. He is awesome! When we think about how awesome He is, we also want to be like Him!
Mr. Hebron

WE GLORIFY YOUR NAME

Lord, we glorify Your Name
O Lord, we glorify Your Name
We give You glory, honor
Worship and praise
We glorify Your Name

As one around Your Throne
We lift You up and we exalt You
Almighty God and King
Forever You reign
We glorify Your Name

4

WE MAGNIFY YOU Discovery Collection: Workbook 4

Lord, we glorify Your Name

When we say, **"Lord, we glorify Your Name,"** we are saying that we recognize and accept God's perfect nature, His character and His holiness.

We are also saying that we are committed to living our lives in a way that reflects His character and His nature.

To glorify His name is to praise and honor Him and to live our lives in a way that ALWAYS pleases Him!

> **Philippians 2:9-10**
>
> *So, God lifted Him (Jesus) up to the highest place. God gave Him the Name that is above every name. When the Name of Jesus is spoken, everyone will kneel down to worship Him. Everyone in heaven and on earth and under the earth will kneel down to worship Him.*

6

Yahweh	The Ruler of all things and all people
Creator	God with us
Saviour	Our Lord and Master
King of Kings	Maker of everything
Almighty	Powerful beyond compare
Shepherd	He guides us on the right path and keeps us safe
Emmanuel	Our Rescuer who took us out of darkness and brought us into light

WE MAGNIFY YOU Discovery Collection: Workbook 4

When you want to give someone a gift, do you just throw it into any old bag you find and toss it to them? Or, do you wrap it in beautiful gift paper or place it in a gift bag, and present it with a smile?

When we **give God glory, honor, worship and praise,** we want to present it to Him with a willing and joyful heart.

God is so happy when we do that. It's like wrapping a lovely gift and offering it to Him!

WE MAGNIFY YOU Discovery Collection: Workbook 4

Find the words in **BOLD** (they are hidden in the word search puzzle below) that describe how we give God glory when we praise Him.

You are **GREAT** and **POWERFUL**, **GLORIOUS**, **SPLENDID**, and **MAJESTIC**. Everything in **HEAVEN** and earth is **YOURS**, and You are **KING**, **SUPREME RULER** over all.

1 Chronicles 29: 11, 13

T	U	I	P	I	G	L	S	D	U	J	M	C	N
P	O	W	E	R	F	U	L	O	A	T	J	L	E
G	W	U	E	D	A	T	E	A	Y	I	G	E	V
G	U	E	I	L	U	S	M	A	O	V	K	S	A
L	O	V	E	A	M	S	E	L	U	T	I	I	E
O	U	S	A	D	A	P	R	E	R	U	E	C	H
R	A	U	E	I	O	H	P	S	S	W	L	I	U
I	E	I	U	D	F	P	U	U	G	N	S	T	P
O	I	J	E	N	Y	U	S	R	L	G	N	S	A
U	Y	K	I	E	R	E	G	U	U	R	O	E	P
S	W	I	U	L	L	I	U	L	E	E	E	J	K
E	S	N	N	P	E	U	A	E	E	A	C	A	F
P	E	G	I	S	I	J	S	R	C	T	J	M	E
M	L	I	N	D	I	R	L	P	T	E	R	N	U

WE MAGNIFY YOU Discovery Collection: Workbook 4

As one around Your Throne

We lift You up and we exalt You

A king sits on a throne – a special chair that only kings use. The king is usually surrounded by his most trusted, faithful and loyal supporters!

When we sing about being **as one around Your throne,** we are telling God we recognize that **He is Lord,** and we surround Him with our faithfulness, our obedience and our love.

As one means we are doing this together – as a global people – standing before Him as one, united by our faith in Jesus Christ.

Look at the map below - can you find your country?

Color the picture showing how we are all connected across the world in worshipping God!

WE MAGNIFY YOU Discovery Collection: Workbook 4

When we say, **"We lift You up and we exalt You,"** we're not actually trying to pick God up!

Lift You up means to elevate or to put God at the highest place of focus and priority in our hearts and minds; He is first and most important.

To **exalt** is to raise to a higher rank or position than other things.

When we lift up God and exalt Him, we are saying how great God is, and how much we love and honor Him.

We are declaring, "Wow, God You are great! There is no one like You! We love You, God!"

Use the secret code to find a hidden phrase from the song:

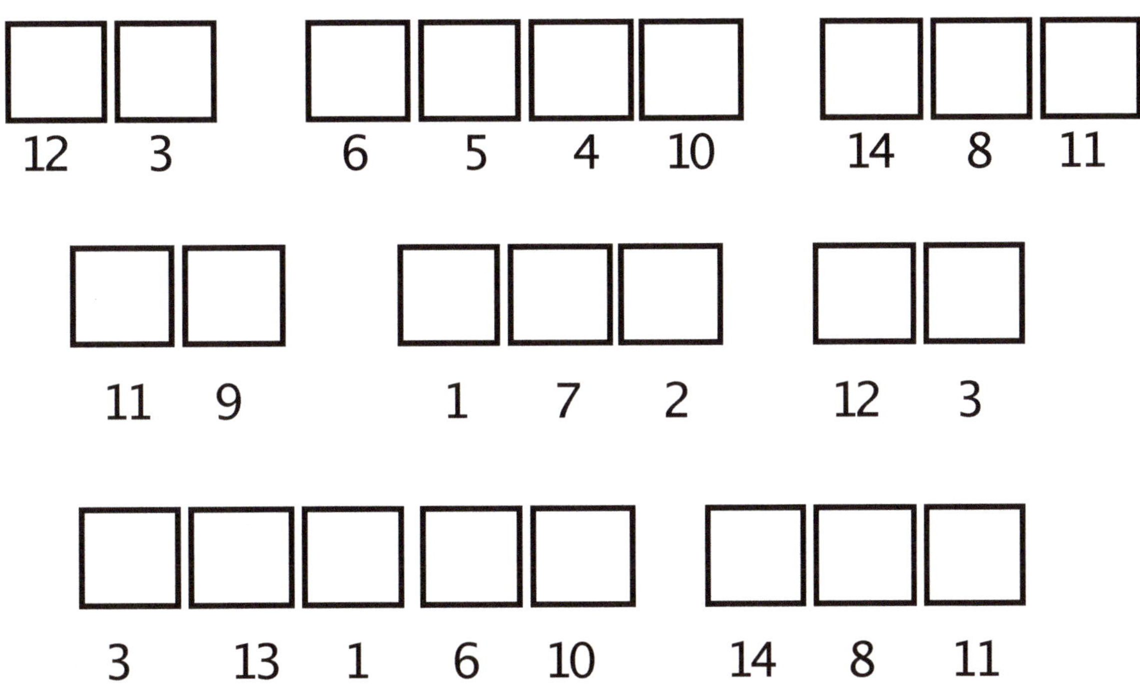

Be sure to share what you discovered!

Secret Code

A	D	E	F	I	L	N	O	P	T	U	W	X	Y
1	2	3	4	5	6	7	8	9	10	11	12	13	14

God is Almighty! Do you know what that means?

Think of the strongest super heroes you've ever heard of—as many as you can. God is more powerful than all of them put together! There is no one who can compete with Him.

He tamed lions to protect Daniel; parted the ocean so Moses and the Israelites could escape the Egyptians; and defeated armies to save David. He even gave Samson super strength, and Esther the wisdom to save her people.

God is our King! He is able to give us whatever we need to fulfill His will for our lives —boldness when we're afraid; wisdom to make right choices; and strength and protection to remain on the course He has set for our lives!

God can do this because He is Almighty and He is King!

God is the Almighty! He's better than all superheroes put together!

In each of the stars, write or draw the **SUPERPOWERS** God has given to you!

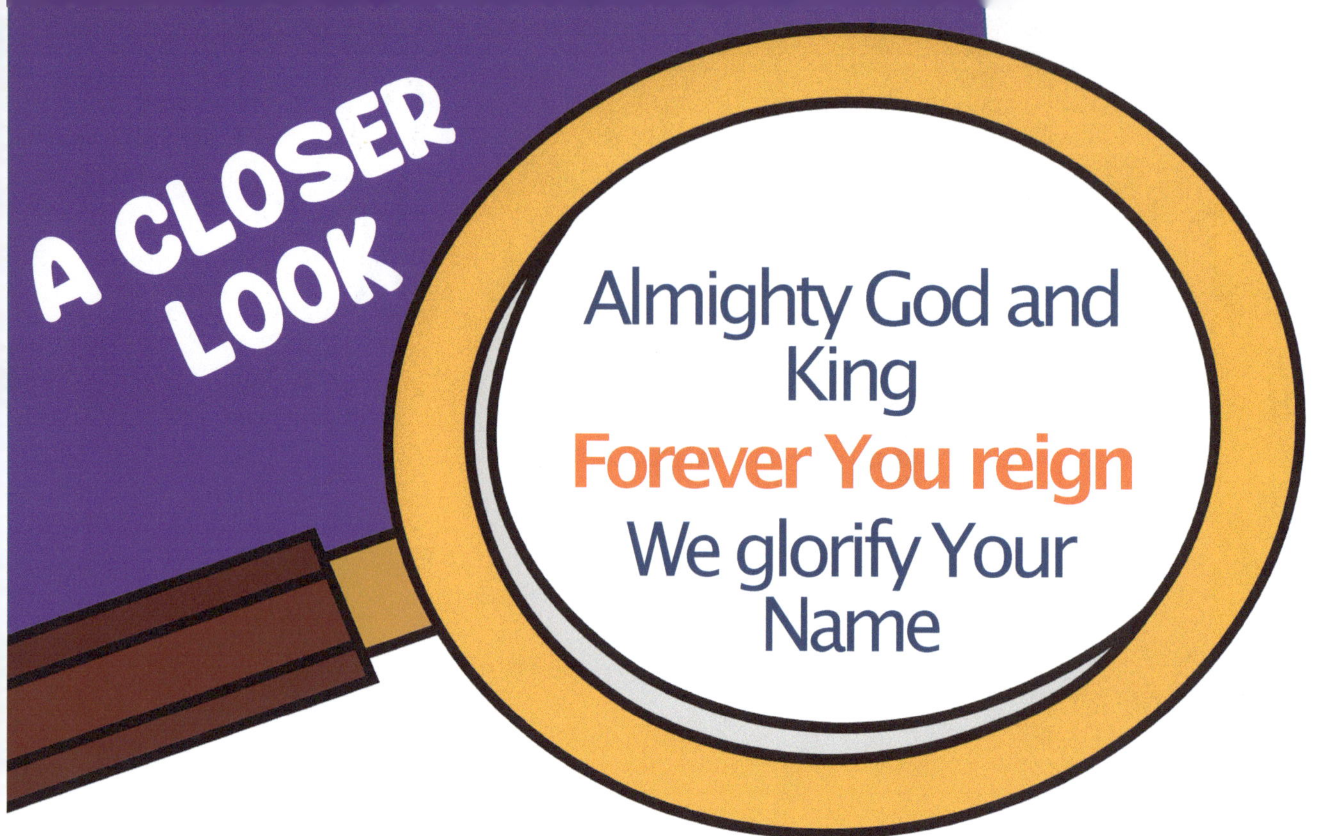

God reigns forever!

Reign is the length of time a king rules his kingdom. In this song, we say that God is King of Kings FOREVER. That is, for all time, and into eternity!

He will never be replaced like the kings, presidents, or prime ministers of the earth.

Forever You reign means that no one can tell God His time as King of Kings is up. We can feel safe and confident knowing that God will never leave us. He will always be our God and our King.

WE MAGNIFY YOU Discovery Collection: Workbook 4

God reigns FOREVER!

Unscramble the words below to dig into
God's forever-ness!

ALTENRE

___ ___ ___ ___ ___ ___ ___

VEENR EINNDG

___ ___ ___ ___ ___   ___ ___ ___ ___ ___

PPBNTEOLAUS

___ ___ ___ ___ ___ ___ ___ ___ ___ ___ ___

WALAYS

___ ___ ___ ___ ___ ___

ANSWER: ETERNAL, NEVER ENDING, UNSTOPPABLE, ALWAYS

Think about the ways you glorify the Lord, in your praise and in your everyday life! These might be things you choose to do or say.

See if you can think of 7 different ways that start with the letters in the word 'Glorify'!

G

L

O

R

I

F

Y

GOD IS THE ALMIGHTY KING!

Connect the dots below to reveal a picture that reminds us of this.

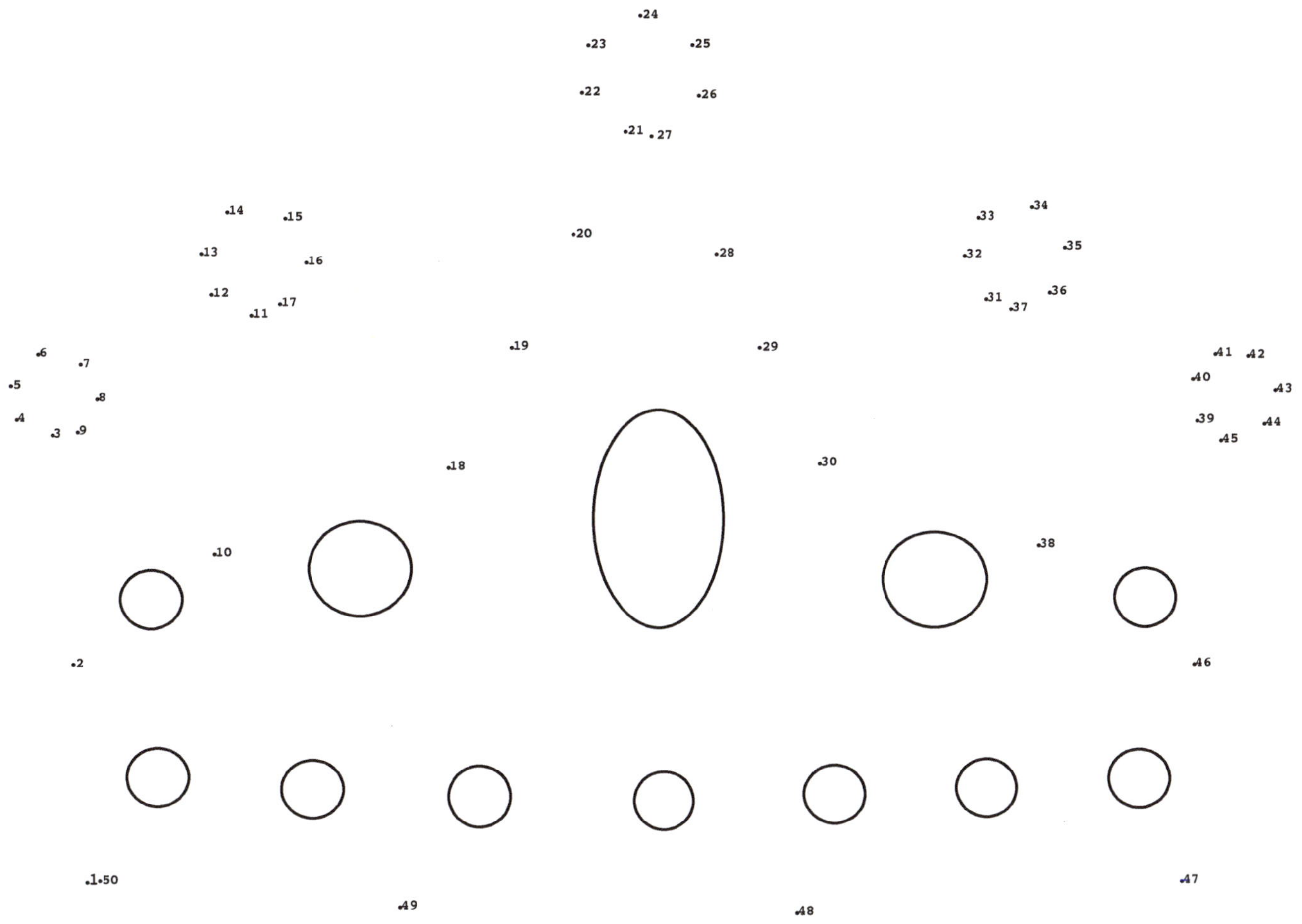

Who is He, this King of glory?
The Lord Almighty — He is the King of glory.
Psalm 24:10

Take some time to reflect on this song. Here's some space to write down your thoughts.

MY JOURNAL

5
BEHOLD
THE LORD
WE MAGNIFY YOU
DISCOVERY COLLECTION

Ms. Charis, can we go on a trip to see God's throne? That would be amazing! We keep singing about it—when can we see it?
Levi
I bet it's HUGE, and covered in diamonds and rubies, with gold arches and sparkly silver...
Abigail
Ms Charis
Children—His throne is right here! We can't see God with our eyes. He rules all things from the spirit realm, which is unseen.
Wherever God is in charge, that's His throne room. We are in His throne room whenever we obey, serve or worship Him.

BEHOLD THE LORD

Behold the Lord on His throne
King of Kings and Lord of Lords
For His Kingdom is everlasting
His power and majesty endure

We magnify You
Place none before You
We glorify and bless Your Holy Name
Behold Your honor
Your saints together
Offering to You the highest praise

Behold He reigns forevermore
Glorious One whom we adore
From age to age unchanging
Who was and is and is to come

Behold the Lamb, Son of God
Conquering King and Lord of all
Sound Your trumpets, judge the nations
Let all know the Lord Almighty reigns

Read, color and learn the verse below:

God rules over the nations. He is seated on His holy throne. Psalm 47 v 8

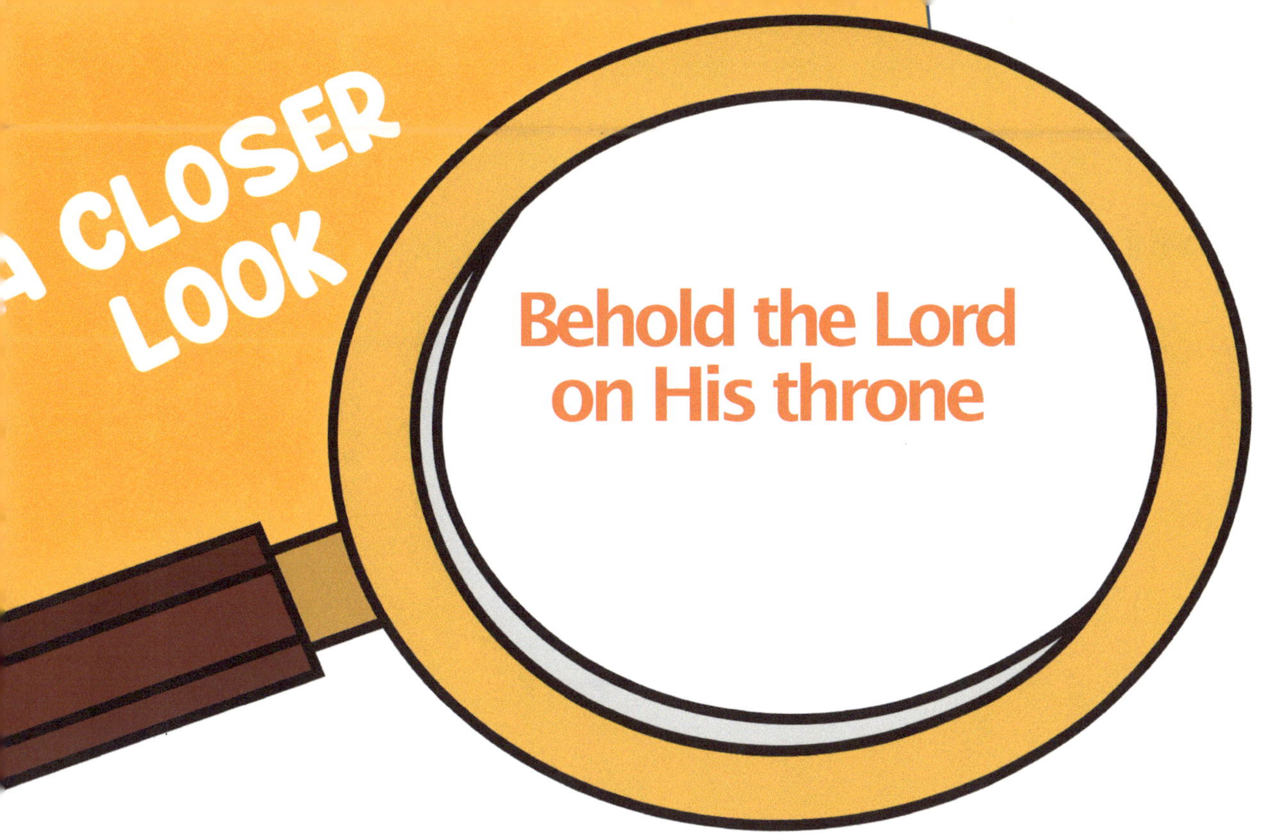

Behold the Lord on His throne

Behold is like saying, "Wow! Look!"

We are fixing our eyes on something amazing and spectacular, and we want to take it all in!

So, when we say, **"Behold, the Lord on His throne,"** we stop what we are doing and look up at God with respect and wonder. We give Him our fullest attention because He is our King and Lord!

WE MAGNIFY YOU Discovery Collection: Workbook 5

The image of a crown helps us remember the words of the song, about how God is our conquering King.

WE MAGNIFY YOU Discovery Collection: Workbook 5

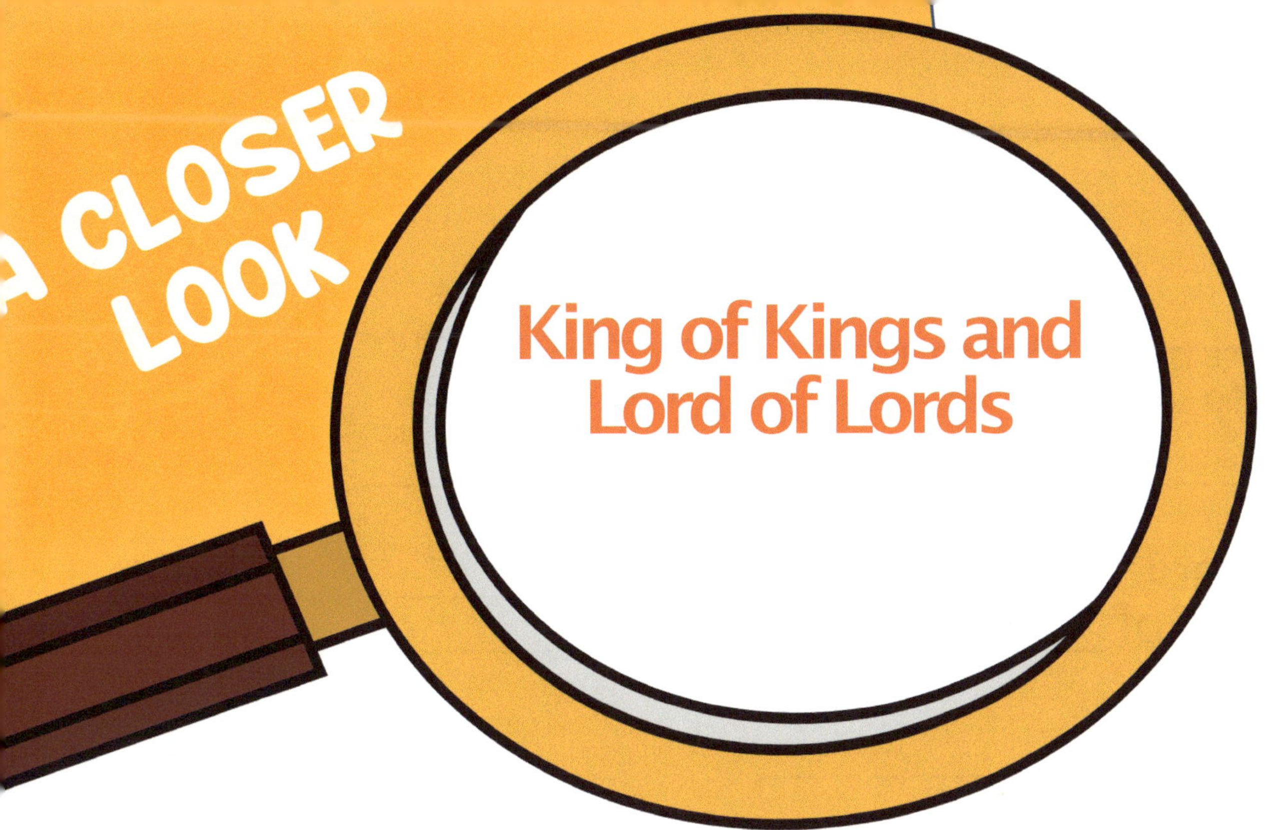

A king is a leader, like a president or prime minister, who is in charge of a nation.

Our God is not an ordinary king. **God is the King of Kings, and Lord of Lords** - which means He ranks higher than all human rulers.

When we declare this, it reminds us of who's really in charge of EVERYTHING!

When we worship we make declarations about the Lord as ruler of all!

Fill in the blanks with the missing words from the song.

Behold the __________ on His ________
King of ________ and Lord of __________

The place a king rules is called his kingdom. **God's Kingdom is everlasting** - that means it cannot be destroyed, and it does not get old or fall apart.

His power and majesty endure - we're speaking about a powerful God! He created the universe, our planet and He created man.

His **majesty** is the beauty of God displayed across His creation, from the stars in the sky, to everything in the earth - the birds, the trees, the animals and even the tiniest of creatures. His majesty remains constant and will never fade away!

Write your own words or sentences for each letter of ENDURE, to help you think about what God's enduring and everlasting Kingdom means.

E
N
D
U
R
E

Your Kingdom is a Kingdom that will last forever.
Your rule will continue for all time to come.
Psalm 145:13a

Behold He reigns forevermore

Did you remember that **behold** means to stop and look, in amazement and wonder?

As we **behold** Him, we see that God is the King of Kings, and that He reigns in Heaven and on the earth. He is a great God—He will never stop doing what He does. He is in charge of the heavens and the earth, He is in charge of our lives, and He will **reign forevermore!**

When something is **glorious** it is beautiful and stunning to look at. God is the **glorious One** the song is talking about.

Adore means to love deeply. When we think of who God is, what He is like, and all He has done, it's easy for us to adore Him.

Think of your family members who lived long before you were born: your parents, your grandparents, your great-grandparents, your great- great- great- great- great- great- grandparents...!

When we think of many generations stretched out over time, we are thinking of **age to age**.

God has always existed and He remains the same; He is **unchanging**. He is the same faithful, powerful God, forever. From before the earth was created, to when your great-great-great-great-great-great grandparents were here... right up to today, God rules!

Who was and is and is to come - He was here yesterday, He is still here today, He will be there tomorrow, and He will be there beyond the end of time!

Match the scrambled words on the LEFT
to the correct words on the RIGHT.

Remember to find out what they mean!

HBLDOE	EVERLASTING
OHERNT	GLORIOUS
IGRLSOOU	BEHOLD
DROAE	SAINTS
GIMOKDN	THRONE
LISEAVGRNTE	KINGDOM
IANTSS	TOGETHER
EEHTOGTR	ADORE

WE MAGNIFY YOU Discovery Collection: Workbook 5

To **magnify** God is to declare that He is the greatest in the whole universe!

When we **magnify** God, we are saying that we make Him the biggest and best thing in our lives.

We **place none before You** means that God is more important than anyone or anything else!

16

Use the clues to solve the crossword puzzle.

ACROSS:
2. Jesus is the ___ of God
4. Blow this to signal the king's arrival
6. King of Kings and Lord of _____
9. Never–ending, like God's Kingdom
12. Rules, e.g. over a Kingdom

DOWN:
1. Who was and is __ ____
3. To last forever, like God's power and majesty
5. The same from age to age
7. God will judge them
8. What we offer to God
10. We bless Your holy ____
11. Behold the Lord on His _____

WE MAGNIFY YOU Discovery Collection: Workbook 5

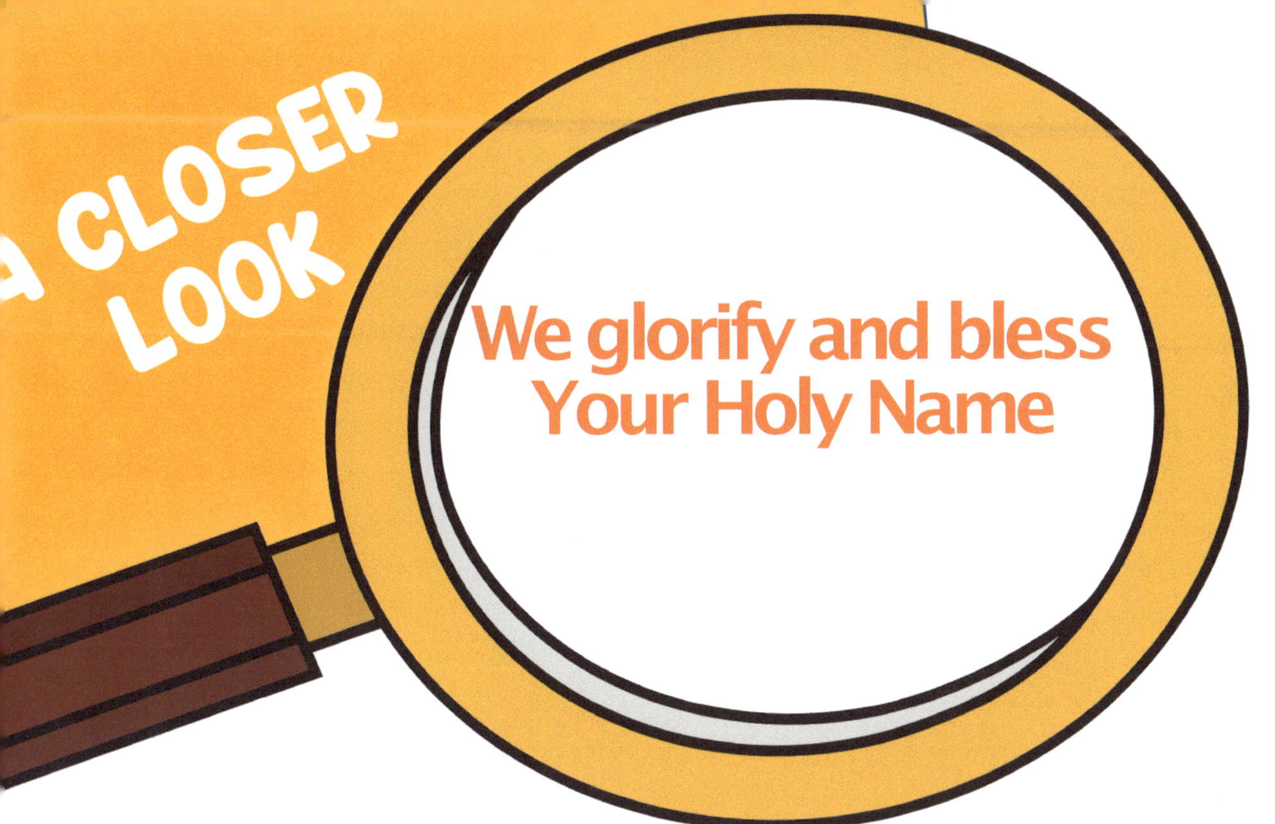

God's Name is holy!

When we make the right choices, like loving others, being obedient, praying and studying the Word of God, we **bless His Name**!

We can bring dishonor to God if we don't do what He wants or expects us to do. If we are disobedient, dishonest, rude or unkind - then we are not **blessing His Holy Name**.

So, when we sing, **"We glorify and bless your Holy Name,"** we are telling God that we are committed to making the right choices and always living according to His Word and His will for our lives!

God feels honored when He looks at His **saints together,** reflecting His holy character and nature, obeying His laws, and following His ways. That's us—the body of Christ, singing joyfully and worshipping Him with pure hearts.

We sing, **"Behold Your honor,"** because we understand how marvelous it is for God to see His people, who love each other, all at the same time **offering Him the highest praise!**

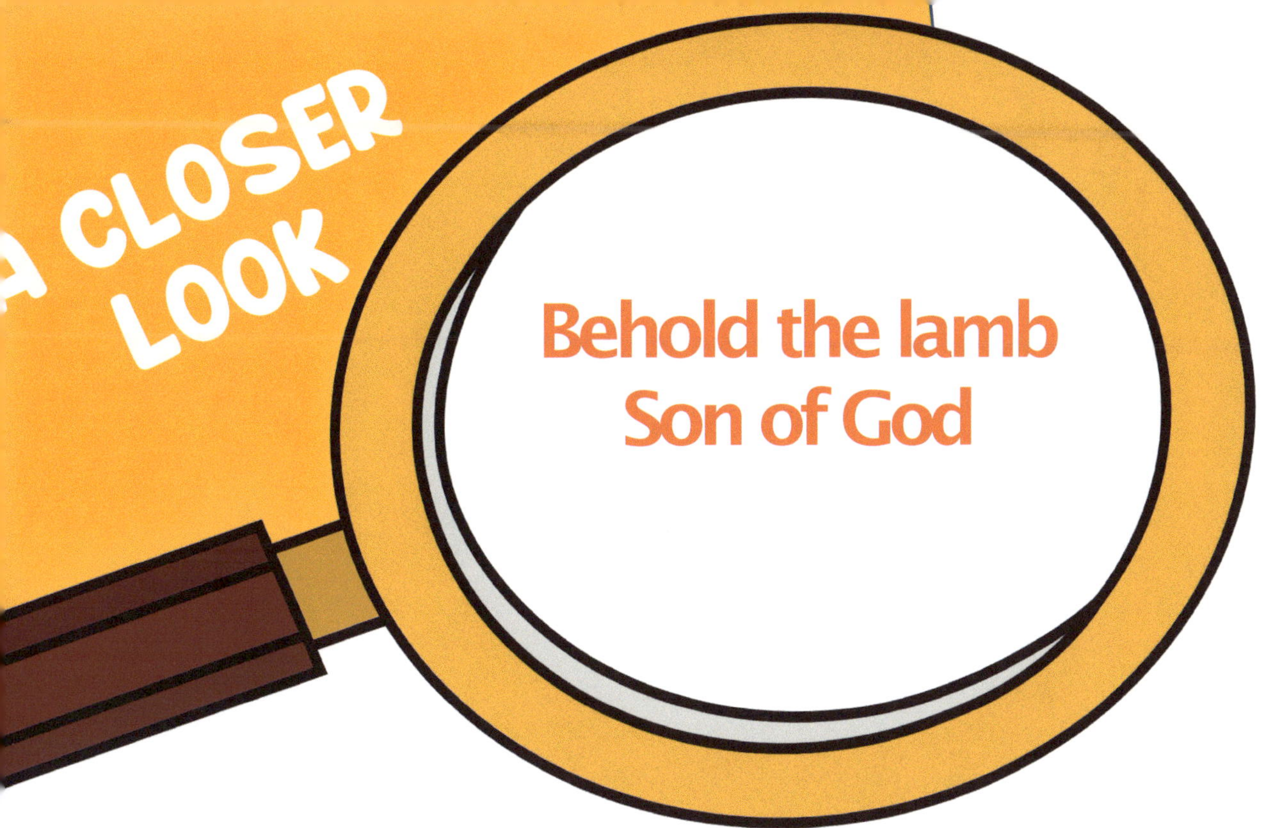

In the Old Testament, God's people would sacrifice their best lamb to God to show their love for Him.

Jesus is called the **Lamb**, because He is the sacrifice God Himself made for all of us to be able to know God. Jesus' sacrifice took our sin away - how amazing!

And there's that word again: **behold -** commanding us to watch and observe Jesus the **Lamb, the Son of God.**

We know that Jesus is our King and He is loving, and holy and just.

But He is also a warrior and has defeated many armies and enemies who tried to stop His people from advancing. So we say He is a **conquering King!**

A king that **conquers** is one who is victorious in battle.

As God leads us to the Finish, we can be assured that He is able to conquer anything that tries to come against Him and the completion of His purpose.

He is **Lord of all!**

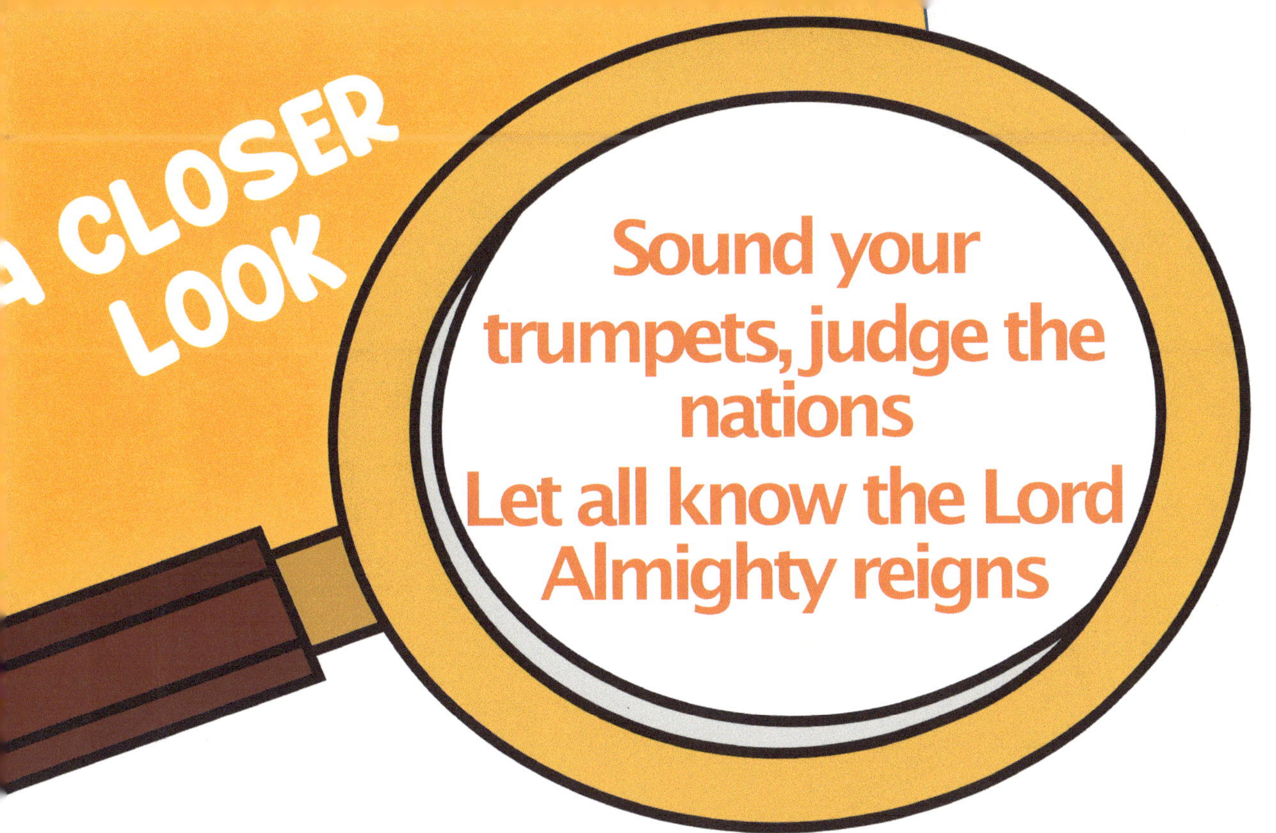

In the Book of Revelation, the sound of trumpets is a signal that God is ready to **judge the nations.**

The **nations** (the countries) of the earth must find out that **the Lord Almighty reigns**. When we obey God and live in His ways, we are bringing judgment to the nations.

Let all know - This is like sending a message to a large group of people - the WHOLE EARTH! It's like sending out an announcement on the Internet, the radio and TV, letting everyone know **the Lord Almighty reigns!**

WE MAGNIFY YOU Discovery Collection: Workbook 5

Take some time to reflect on this song. Here's some space to write down your thoughts.

MY JOURNAL

6
HOLY IS
THE LAMB
WE MAGNIFY YOU
DISCOVERY COLLECTION
HOLY IS THE LAMB
WE MAGNIFY YOU
DISCOVERY WORKBOOK
6

Levi, did you know that thousands of people are singing these same worship songs across the whole world?

But how can they, when we speak different languages? And it's night-time on the other side of the world right now!

We are one holy nation singing God's praise, in different languages, but yet with one voice. What's even more interesting is we are singing some of the same songs that the angels surrounding God's throne sing! Now, that's glorious!

Abigail

Levi

HOLY IS THE LAMB

LYRICS

Holy, Holy,
Holy is the Lamb
Lord God Almighty
Who was and is
Who was and is
Who was and is to come

All creation gives You glory
With all our hearts we bless Your Name
From every language, tribe and nation
Your holy people sing Your praise

We bow before Your holy presence
We lift our hands and worship You
Lord, You alone deserve this honor
You alone deserve all praise
All praise

4

Holy, holy, holy is the Lord God Almighty, who was, and is, and is to come."

Revelation 4:8

Jesus is the Lamb of God!

A lamb is a young sheep—but what does Jesus have in common with a sheep?

Long ago, people honored God by giving Him their best lamb. They would place the lamb on an altar as a sacrifice—to say sorry for their sins, or to let God know how thankful they were about something.

Holy means sacred and set apart for a special purpose. The lamb was the perfect sacrifice, because it represented something that was pure, innocent and precious.

Jesus is the **Holy Lamb** because He was without sin; He was innocent. He gave His life as a sacrifice for us so that all who believe in Him and follow His ways could enter the Kingdom of God.

Can you unscramble these words?
Do you know what they mean?

LFOYGRI

_ _ _ _ _ _ _

ONROH

_ _ _ _ _

ROETHN

_ _ _ _ _ _

XTEAL

_ _ _ _ _

NRGIE

_ _ _ _ _

ERVROEF

_ _ _ _ _ _ _

ANSWER: GLORIFY, HONOR, THRONE, EXALT, REIGN, FOREVER

WE MAGNIFY YOU Discovery Collection: Workbook 6

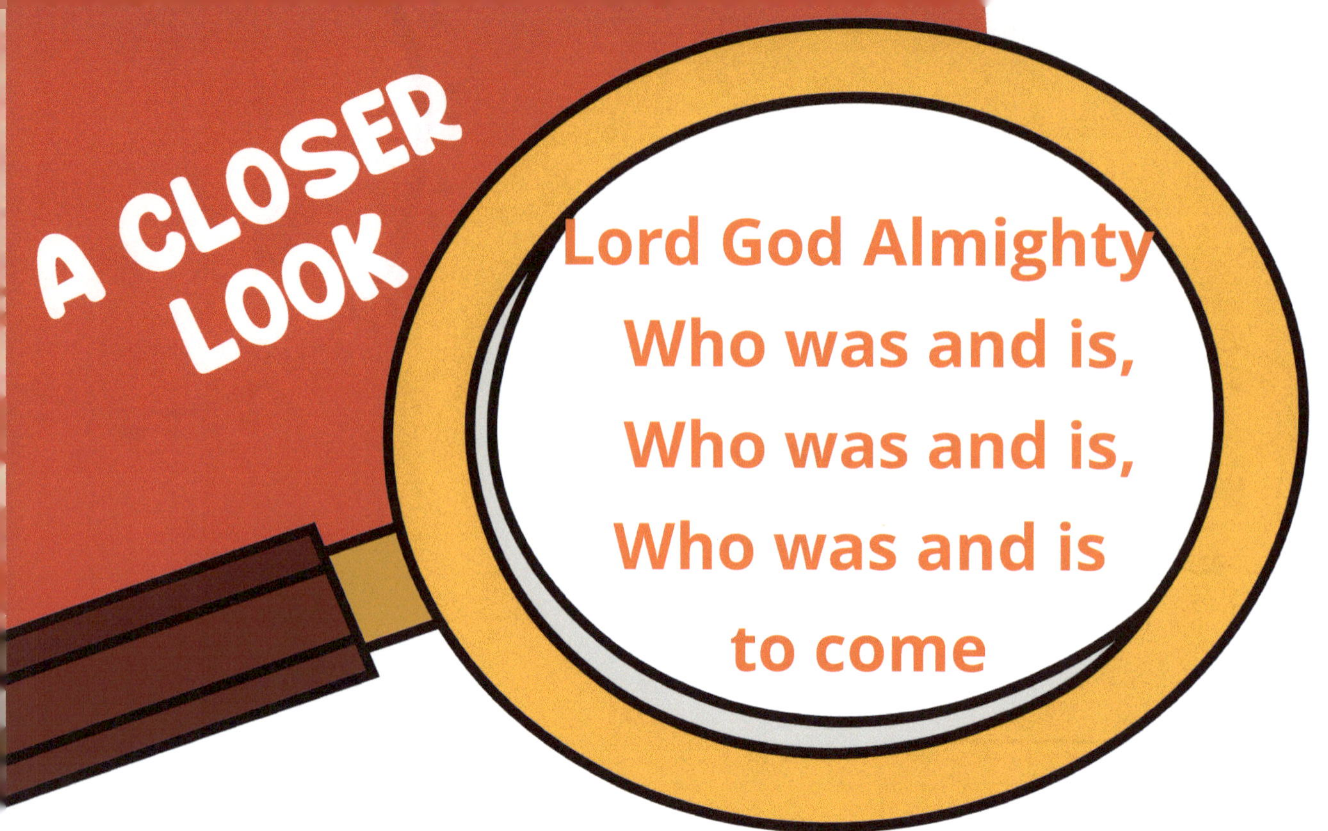

Our Lord is the **Lord God Almighty!**

That means He is stronger than the strongest super heroes, and more powerful than the world's most powerful armies. He can defeat any enemy! No one is stronger or more powerful than Him!

Who was, and is and is to come simply means that God existed before we were born; He is with us today, and He will be with us tomorrow. In fact, He is eternal. That means He will be around forever!

God does not exist in time like us.

In the first box below, draw a picture of yourself when you were younger. Then draw yourself now in the second box. Next, imagine how you might look in the future and draw the future you in box #3.

God doesn't have to imagine the future, He knows it already!

Revelation 1:8

"I am the First and the Last," says the Lord God Almighty, who is, who was, and who is to come.

Creation is everything God has made, like the sky, stars, plants, rivers, insects, birds, animals and trees. God made all of this!

When we look at creation and see the beauty of a flower in bloom, or how animals hunt, or how birds soar in the sky... we can see how awesome God, our creator, is!

In other words, **God's creation gives Him glory,** just like we do in our worship.

Everything on earth will worship You; they will sing Your praises, shouting Your name in glorious songs.

Psalm 66:4

Can you find your way from the Beginning (ALPHA) to the End (OMEGA)?

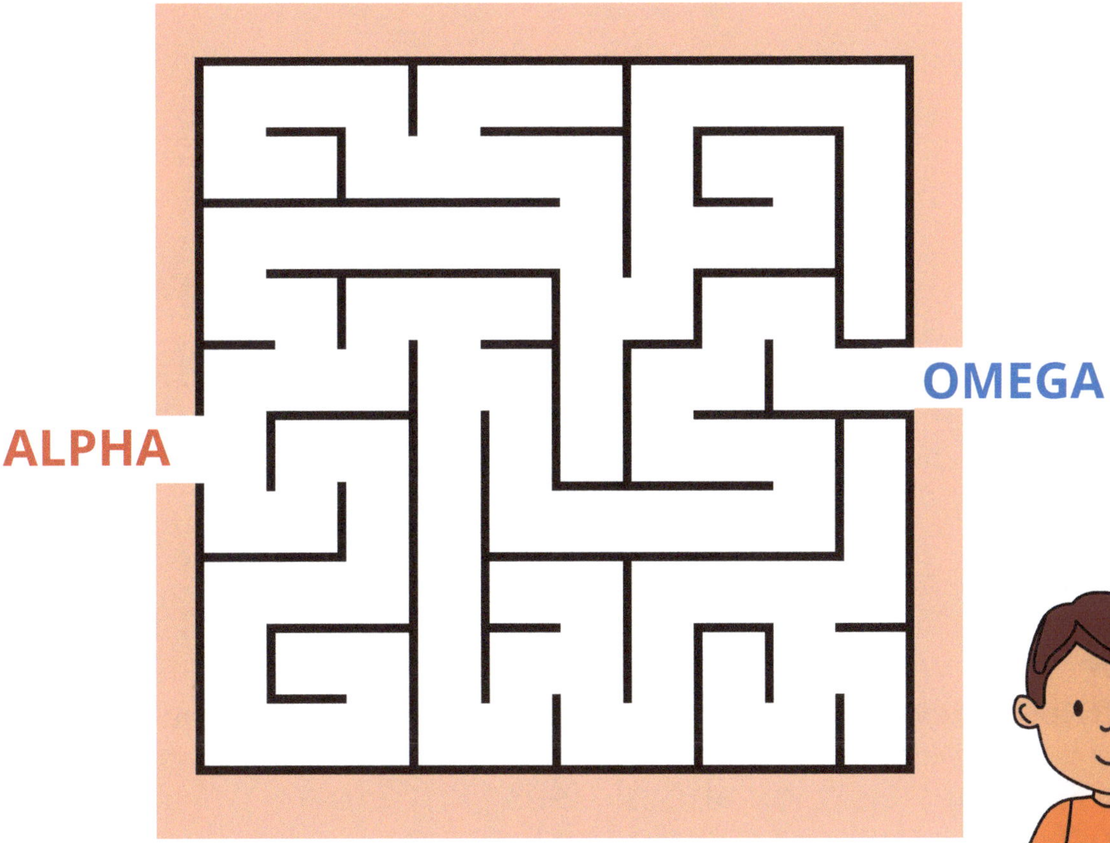

I am the Alpha and the Omega, the First and the Last, the Beginning and the End.

Revelation 22:13

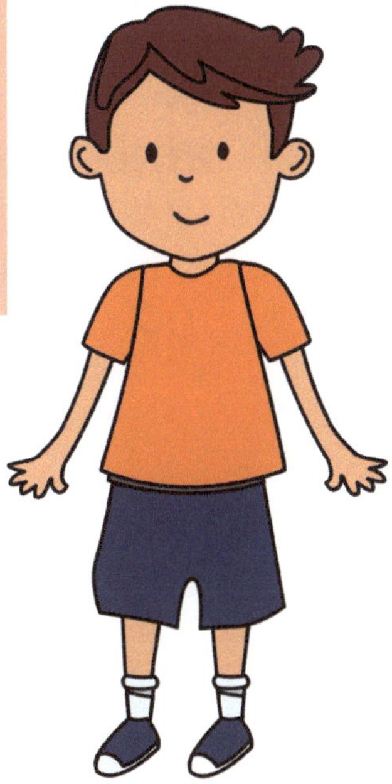

With all our hearts does not mean that you have more than one heart in your body!

In fact, this phrase reminds us that we are part of a global civilization, each lifting our heart to the Lord, to praise and bless His name together.

When we sing, **"We bless Your name,"** we are saying, "We are praising and worshipping You God, because we know that you are awesome, majestic and sovereign Lord!"

This brings God joy and blesses Him. How incredible that we can do this!

Find these hidden words in the puzzle below:

- ☐ LORD
- ☐ PRAISE
- ☐ ALMIGHTY
- ☐ PRESENCE
- ☐ PEOPLE
- ☐ CREATION
- ☐ SING
- ☐ BLESS
- ☐ LAMB
- ☐ NATION
- ☐ TRIBE
- ☐ HOLY
- ☐ AGE
- ☐ DECADE
- ☐ TIME
- ☐ DAY
- ☐ MONTH
- ☐ YEAR
- ☐ ETERNAL
- ☐ EVERLASTING

L	D	T	S	E	R	S	C	N	A	T	I	O	N
P	R	A	I	S	E	Y	L	D	B	Y	E	R	A
O	E	I	G	N	P	T	A	E	L	T	A	G	E
R	C	R	E	A	T	I	O	N	S	G	L	A	V
D	A	K	C	Y	O	M	U	C	D	H	M	S	E
E	L	E	R	B	T	E	B	H	A	A	I	T	R
C	B	M	A	L	G	V	E	T	Y	E	G	D	L
A	M	D	T	E	H	E	C	P	S	G	H	E	A
D	I	A	R	S	Y	T	N	L	N	P	T	C	S
E	H	Y	I	S	E	E	E	I	E	A	Y	Q	T
L	O	R	D	F	A	R	S	S	M	I	Z	M	I
N	L	E	B	C	R	N	E	B	I	R	T	O	N
A	Y	P	E	I	O	A	R	Y	H	F	I	N	G
Y	M	O	N	T	H	L	P	E	O	P	L	E	B

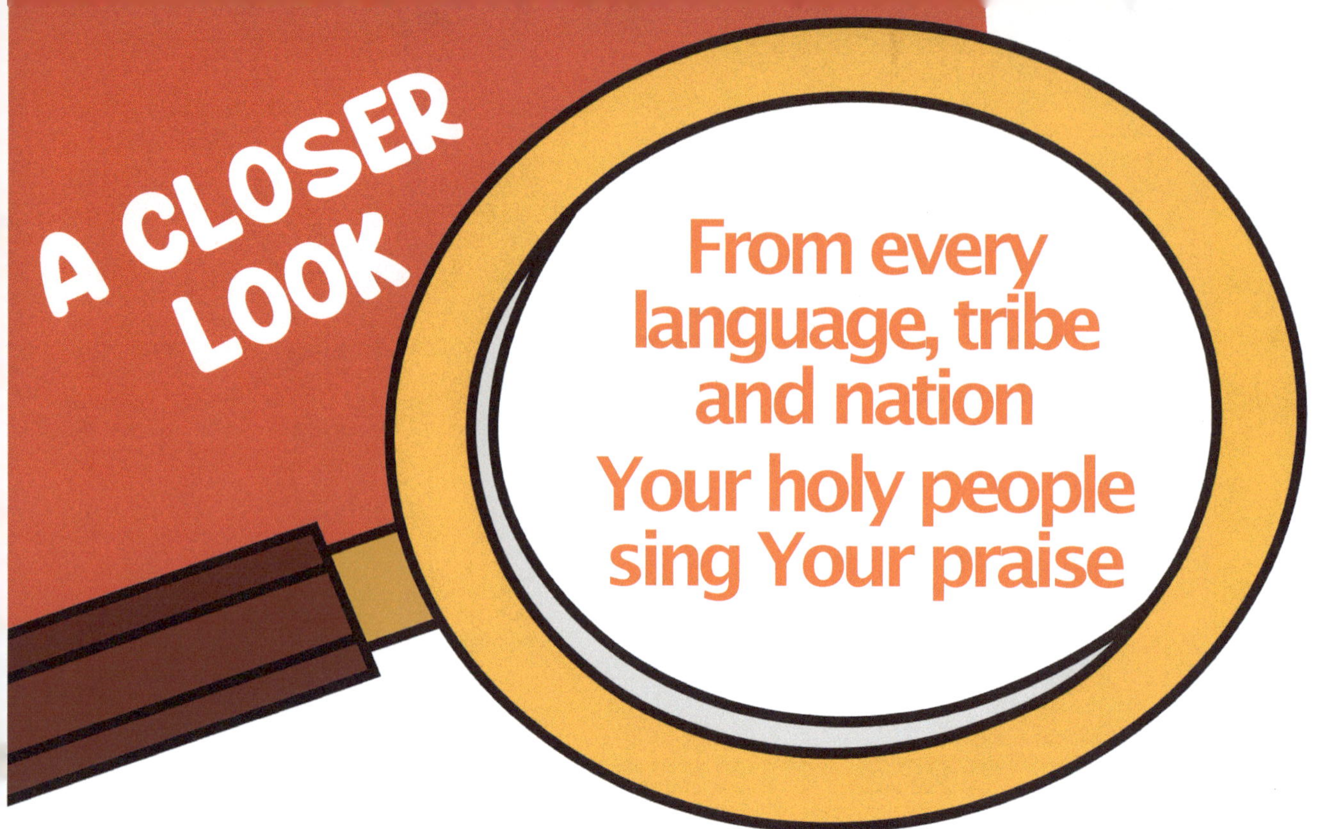

There are millions of people living in different communities all across the earth. Their languages are different, their food is different, their homes are different.

God's word says that every tribe and nation will lift their voices in praise to Him.

After this I looked, and there was an enormous crowd—no one could count all the people! They were from every race, tribe, nation, and language, and they stood in front of the throne and of the Lamb, dressed in white robes and holding palm branches in their hands. They called out in a loud voice: "Salvation comes from our God, who sits on the throne, and from the Lamb!"

Revelation 7:9-10

See if you can match the words 'Holy is the Lamb' with the language it is written in. Then draw a flag of a country where this language is spoken.

Holy is the Lamb   Spanish

Santo es el cordero   Japanese

ቅዱስ ነው   Amharic

k'idusi newi   French

Heilig ist das Lamm   English

saint est l'agneau   German

聖なる子羊   isiZulu

HINT: You can look up the flags online if you don't know them!

WE MAGNIFY YOU Discovery Collection: Workbook 6

In some countries and cultures people bow as a sign of respect and submission.

In the same way, we **bow before** the one true King, God - to let Him know how much we respect and submit to Him. After all, He is the King and Ruler of our lives.

Even when we do not physically **bow** before the Lord, we should always bow in our hearts to His will. This shows God that we recognize Him as Lord of all, ALWAYS!

When **we lift our hands,** we are saying to God, "I give myself to You," or "I surrender to You."

When we **lift our hands and worship** God, we surrender our attention to Him alone.

We give Him our full focus and block out all other distractions around us.

Our worship is an expression of total thankfulness to God, and complete respect for Him.

We also honor our parents and leaders—but our worship is reserved only for God.

Use the secret code to find a hidden phrase from the song.

See if you can use these words the next time you pray.

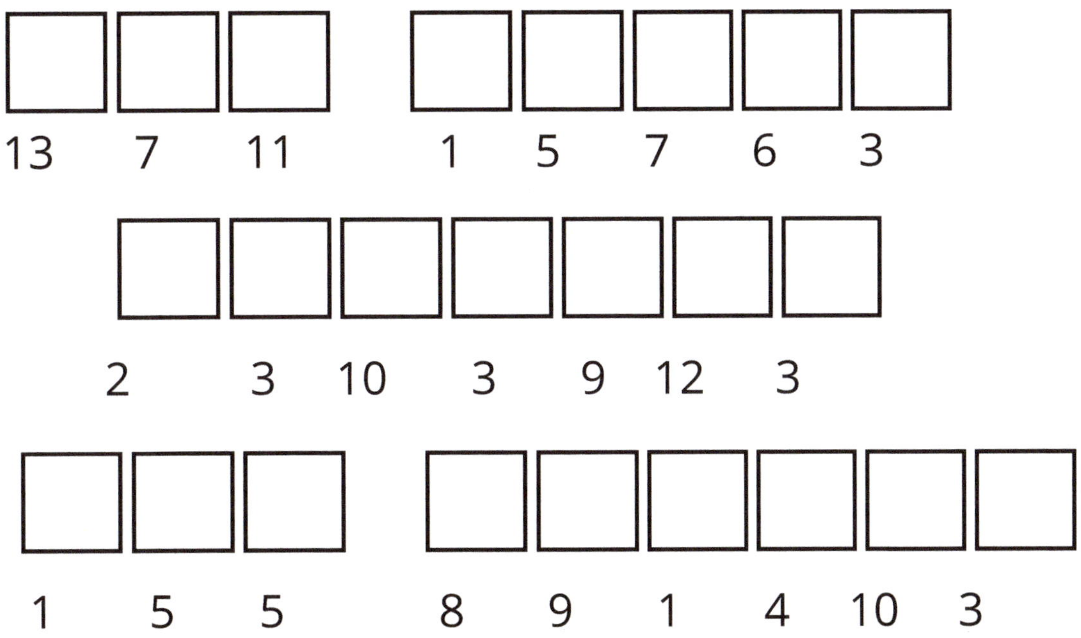

Be sure to share what you discovered!

Secret Code

A	D	E	I	L	N	O	P	R	S	U	V	Y
1	2	3	4	5	6	7	8	9	10	11	12	13

ANSWER: YOU ALONE DESERVE ALL PRAISE

WE MAGNIFY YOU Discovery Collection: Workbook 6

Take some time to reflect on this song. Here's some space to write down your thoughts.

MY JOURNAL

GOD IS HERE (HALLELUJAH)

⑦

WE MAGNIFY YOU
DISCOVERY COLLECTION

Sometimes I hear others say, "Hallelujah," when praying or worshipping, so I say it too... But I don't really know what it means.
Abigail
I know that word! I have read it in the Bible too. It means "Praise the Lord!" or "God be praised."
Levi
That's right, Levi. Did you know it also means that we praise Him with joy? When we worship God, our hearts must be filled with joy because we love Him and we love to praise Him. Let's sing "Hallelujah " together now...
Ms Charis

GOD IS HERE (HALLELUJAH!)

Hallelujah! Hallelujah! Hallelujah!
The Lord our God is here!

You're here among Your people
Your glory now made known
Revealed across the nations
In majesty enthroned

Keep us pure and holy
Take us all the way
Lead us to forever
And forever we will say

Hallelujah! Our Lord God is the King who rules over all. Let us be joyful and glad! Let us give Him glory!

Revelation 19:6-7

Hallelujah is a Hebrew word that means joyfully praise the Lord.

God loves it when we praise and worship Him with joyful hearts. It draws us closer to God, and Him to us.

Our worship allows God to know how we feel about Him. It also allows us to discover and know Him more.

And as we get closer to God, our joy increases and we want to honor Him even more!

Can you unscramble this word?

LUAHLJHLEA

— — — — — — — — — —

ANSWER: HALLELUJAH

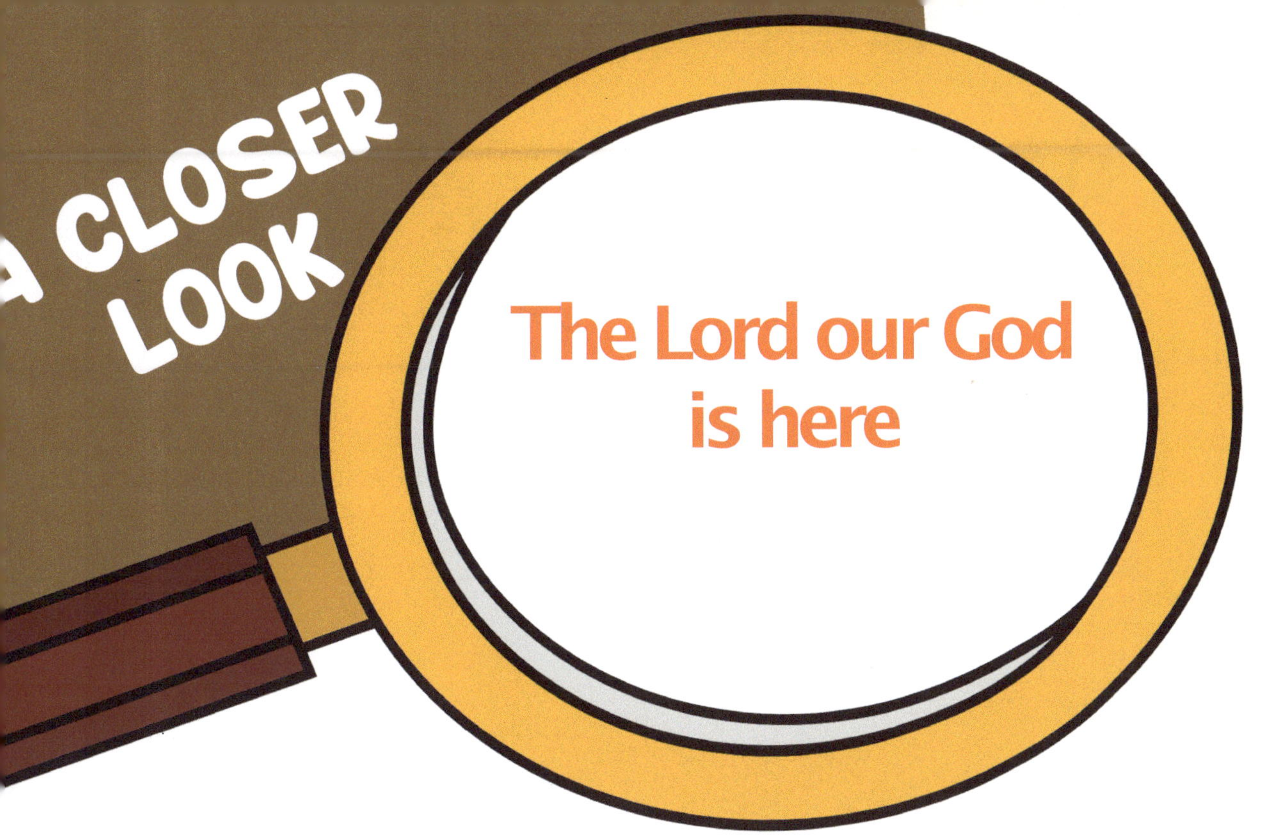

When we refer to God as our **Lord**, we are telling Him - and everyone else - that He is in charge of our lives.

When we declare that **our God is here,** we are acknowledging that is He is not just nearby, He is right beside us!

When our parents or teachers are right beside us, we know we have to be obedient and attentive. So, when God is beside us, we have to show, even more, how much we respect His presence, His authority and His holiness!

Follow the numbers and connect the dots to reveal the hidden picture. What do you see?

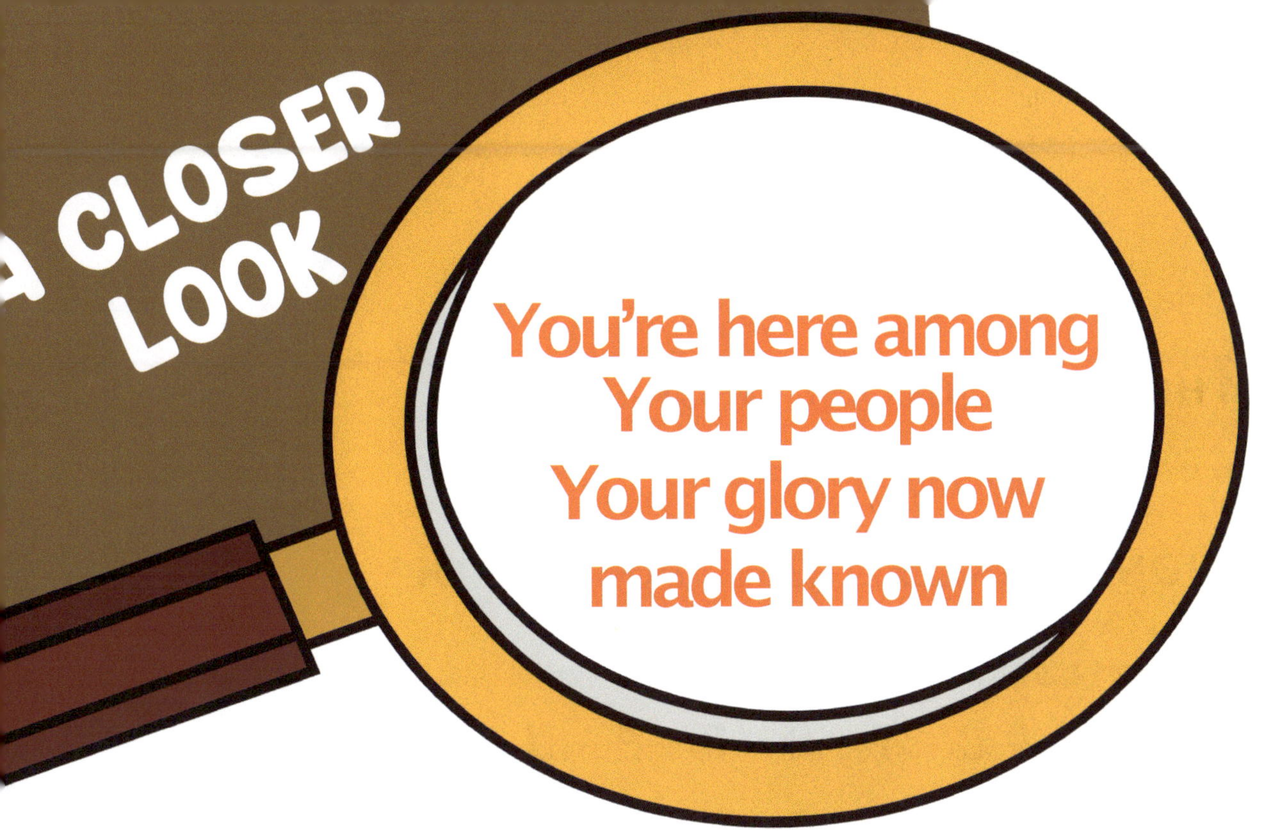

You're here among Your people is the fulfilment of a promise God made a long time ago:

I will make My home with My people and live among them; I will be their God, and they shall be My people.
2 Corinthians 6:16

Your glory now made known. When God looks at His people spread across the whole earth – OBEDIENT, FAITHFUL and PURE – He sees His own character and nature reflected in them – and the world sees it too!

The reason He is with us is because we are His chosen people! We are a global company of people joyfully obeying God's commands. The Bible says this is what God always wanted!

But you are a chosen people, a royal priesthood, a holy nation, God's special possession, that you may declare the praises of Him who called you out of darkness into His wonderful light.

1 Peter 2:9

Find these words from the song hidden in the puzzle below:

☐ **ENTHRONED** ☐ **GLORY** ☐ **FOREVER**

☐ **HERE** ☐ **REVEALED** ☐ **PEOPLE**

☐ **NATIONS** ☐ **HALLELUJAH** ☐ **PURE** ☐ **HOLY**

H	E	A	L	O	T	R	R	E	U	V	O	H	L
U	E	A	E	R	R	O	L	H	R	U	T	O	H
G	E	E	N	T	H	R	O	N	E	D	P	H	L
R	E	L	A	H	E	S	S	Y	D	R	R	S	L
N	O	E	E	E	H	D	D	R	F	E	P	N	H
L	R	A	O	U	A	A	E	S	O	L	S	O	E
S	G	V	R	E	L	J	R	E	R	P	O	I	O
A	L	A	E	N	L	G	E	R	E	O	N	T	N
V	O	H	D	E	E	R	V	E	V	E	L	A	N
U	R	L	P	R	L	L	E	H	E	P	E	N	Y
E	Y	E	E	E	U	E	A	L	R	N	H	E	R
P	L	E	J	O	J	P	L	E	P	U	R	E	F
O	H	E	P	E	A	Y	E	N	E	E	R	E	E
S	L	O	E	R	H	A	D	A	Y	L	O	H	H

To **reveal** something means that it can be seen by others. God's glory is being **revealed across the nations** through us.

How do we reveal His glory?

Every time each of us—wherever we are in the world—makes the choice to:
- **LISTEN** to His Voice
- **OBEY** His Commands
- **BELIEVE** His Word
- **FOLLOW** His Ways
- **FULFILL** His Will for our lives

Psalm 96:3 Declare His glory among the nations, His marvelous deeds among all peoples.

13

A CLOSER LOOK

In majesty enthroned

Majesty is a word used to describe something that is impressive in its beauty, scale and stateliness. That's why it's a perfect word to describe our God.

In majesty enthroned is a way of saying our Lord is a King whose throne represents His AWESOMENESS!

Oh! I get it! So it means our God has power and strength and dominion and might and authority!"

Or you can just say our God is an AWESOME God!

THE LORD IS MAJESTICALLY ENTHRONED!

Decorate this throne to remember God's greatness.

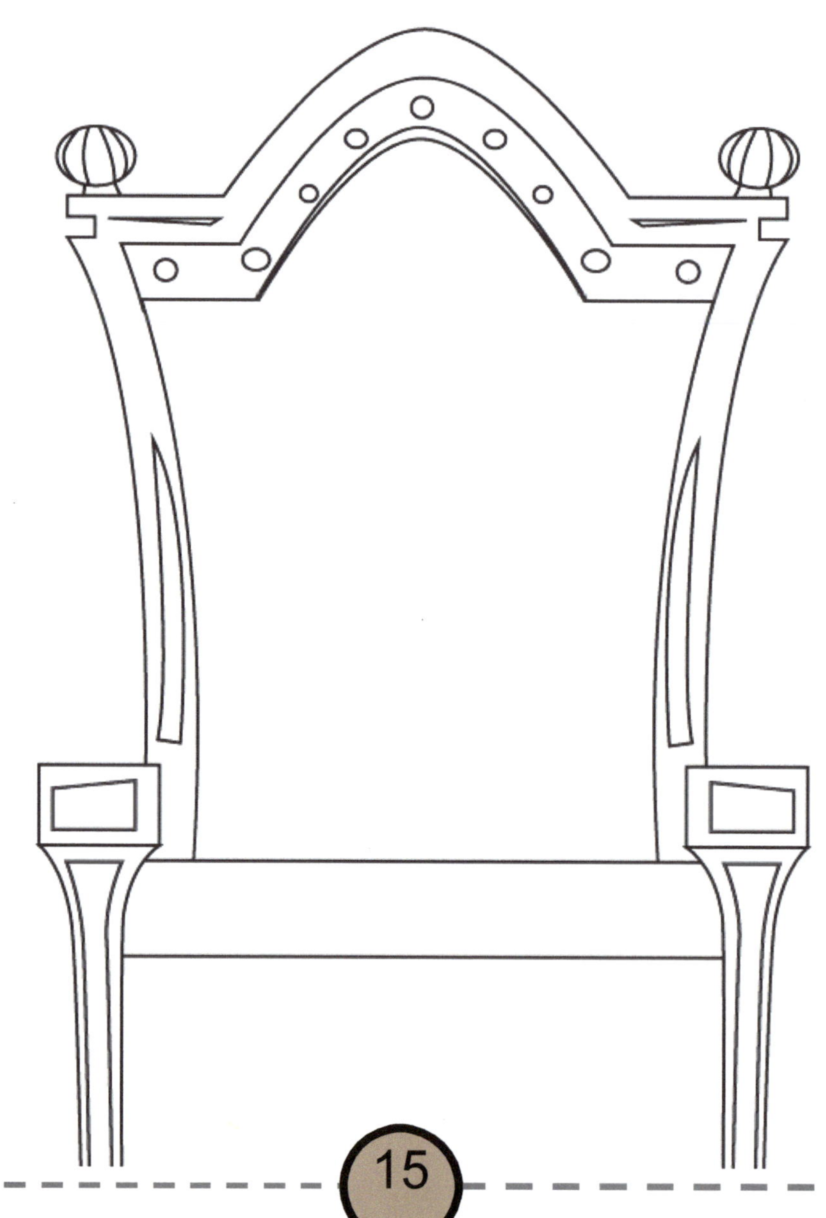

15

Keep us pure and holy

When we say, **"Keep us pure and holy,"** we are asking the Holy Spirit to help us to give us **WISDOM** and **FAITH** and **GRACE** and **LOVE** and **STRENGTH**, so that we can stay away from what's wrong and do what is right to please the Lord.

Use the code to solve 4 hidden words
and phrases that finish the statement:
"Christ has made us..."

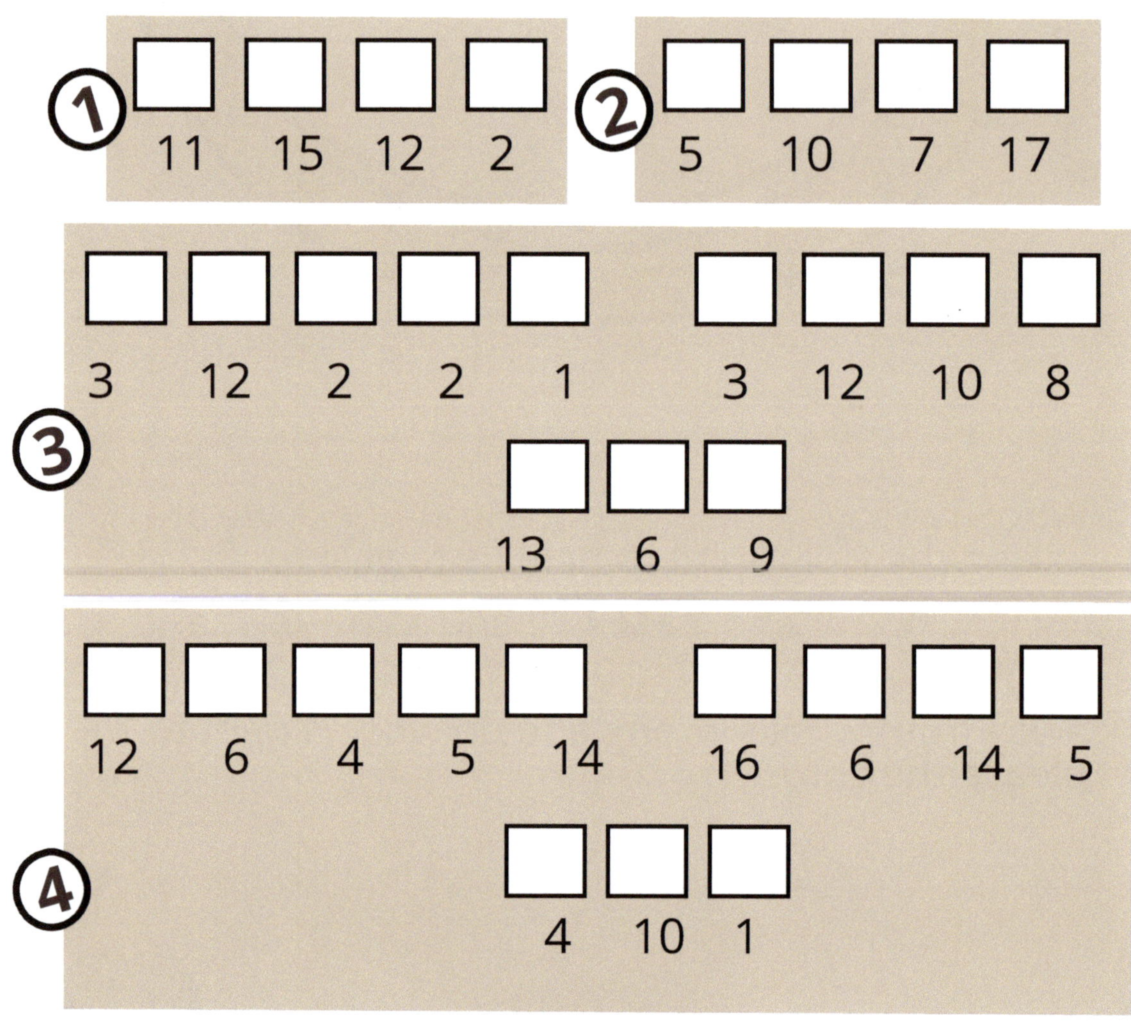

Secret Code

D	E	F	G	H	I	L	M	N	O	P	R	S	T	U	W	Y
1	2	3	4	5	6	7	8	9	10	11	12	13	14	15	16	17

17

ANSWER: PURE, HOLY, FREED FROM SIN, RIGHT WITH GOD

Have you ever run a very long race or done something where you wondered if you could make it all the way to the end?

Well, God has a plan for His Chosen People, His Church. He has a plan for us! We want to FINISH His plan and be with Him!

So our prayer to the Lord is to **take us all the way** to completion of His plan for us and **lead us to forever,** where He is!

Draw a picture of yourself, your family and our global community all running to the finish, to forever!

Write a prayer to thank God for being with us and leading us to Forever!

Take some time to reflect on this song. Here's some space to write down your thoughts.

MY JOURNAL

8

AMEN!

WE MAGNIFY YOU

DISCOVERY COLLECTION

There is another word we use all the time when we pray: "Amen!" – Do you know what it means?
Abigail
That's true. We say it while we pray and at the end. Hmmm... I guess I never really thought much about what it means.
The word "Amen!" communicates our agreement. It means, "Yes! Let it be so!" The song AMEN! is all about our agreement with God's will to complete His purpose for our lives and for the whole earth! Amen!
Levi

AMEN!

You are the God of all creation
All things are under Your command
Bring Your judgment to the nations
Cause Your righteous ones to stand

Amen!
So let it be!
Amen!
Hear our decree!
Let Your Kingdom come
Lord let Your will be done
Now and forevermore
Amen!

Send Your word throughout the nations
Let Your chosen hear Your call
Make us one, Your holy people
Reveal Your glory now to all

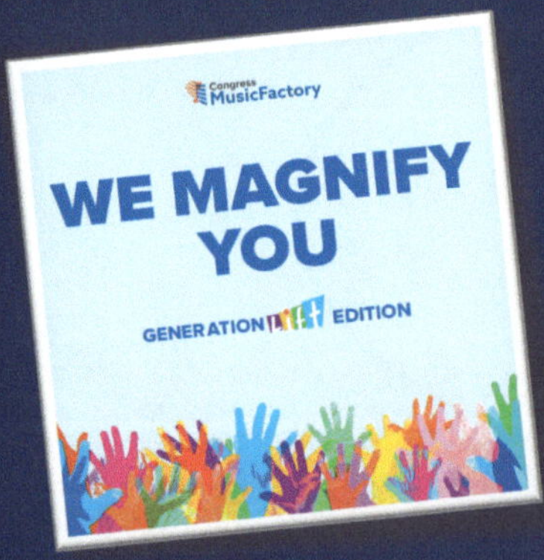

3

Your Kingdom come, Your will be done, on earth as it is in Heaven.

Matthew 6:10

The word **Amen** is actually derived from the Hebrew ā mēn, which means "surely" or "truth". It's a word used to communicate certainty and agreement.

When we declare, **"Amen!"** we are telling God that we agree with His plans and want them to happen!

Decree is another word for declaration or command. A command is given by someone with the right, power or authority to communicate it. As God's children, we have been given the right and authority to make **decrees** on His behalf.

"Hear our decree!" is us telling God to pay attention to us because we agree with His will and we are prepared to help Him to fulfill it.

We have authority - given to us by God - to make decrees. What we decree on earth will be decreed in Heaven.

Jesus says
"I will give you the keys to the Kingdom of Heaven.
What you lock on earth will be locked in Heaven.
What you unlock on earth will be unlocked in Heaven."

Matthew 16: 19

Use the keys below to unlock the padlocks! Draw a line from each key to the padlock it fits:

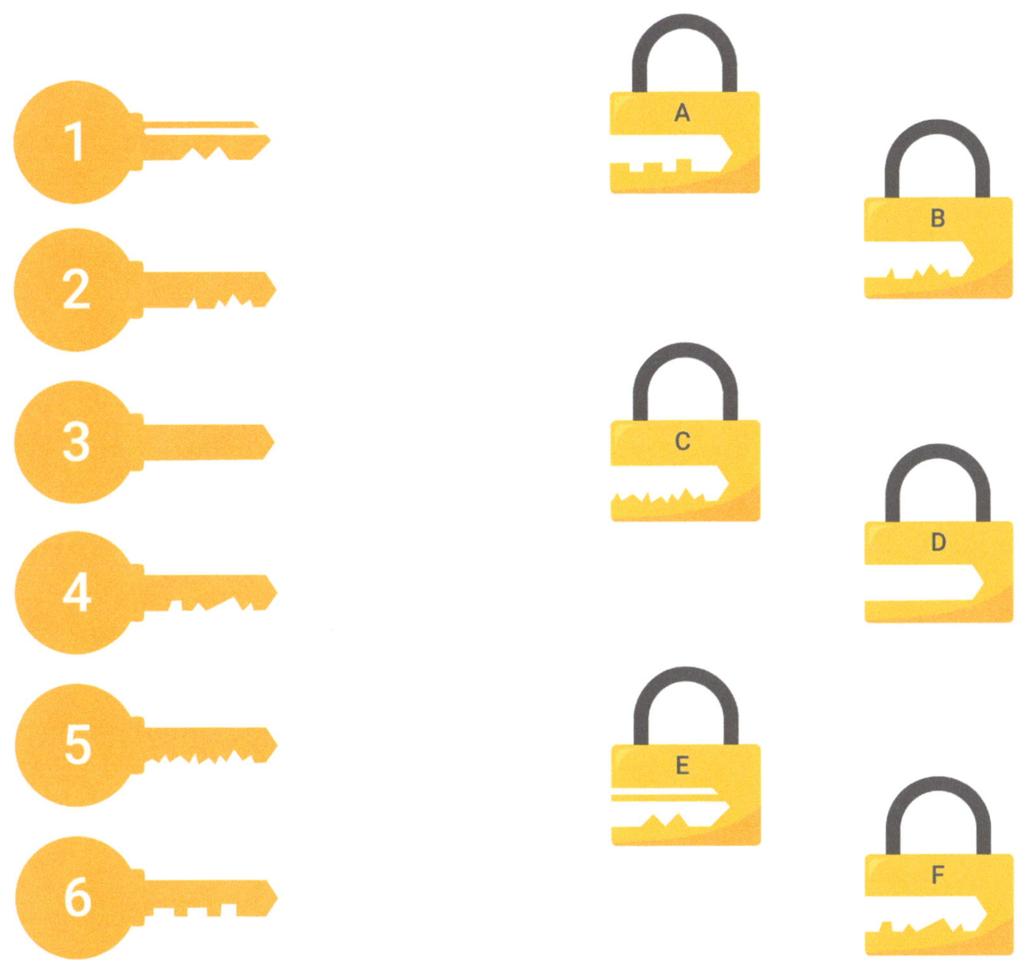

6

When we say, **"Let Your Kingdom come, let Your will be done,"** we are making a decree to the heavens and the earth of our desire to see His laws, His ways and His purpose expressed in our lives.

A kingdom is ruled by a king. Whenever we accept the will of God and obey His command we make Him the King of our life. And when He is the King of our life, His Kingdom come, in us and in the earth – cause that's where we live!

Now and forevermore - tells us that we want everything that God wants, today and always.

> *"... behold, the kingdom of God is within you."*
> *Luke 17:21*

Color the meanings of the word Amen

8

Everything in the world was created by God.

In the book of Genesis in the Bible He commanded the world in to existence.

We are part of God's creation and our job is to do all that He commands!

By the word of the Lord the heavens were made,

And all the host of them by the breath of His mouth...

Psalm 33:6

Color the picture.

- How many fish can you count?
- How many starfish can you spot?
- Do you see any other sea-creatures?

Job 12:10

It is God who directs the lives of His creatures, everyone's life is in His power.

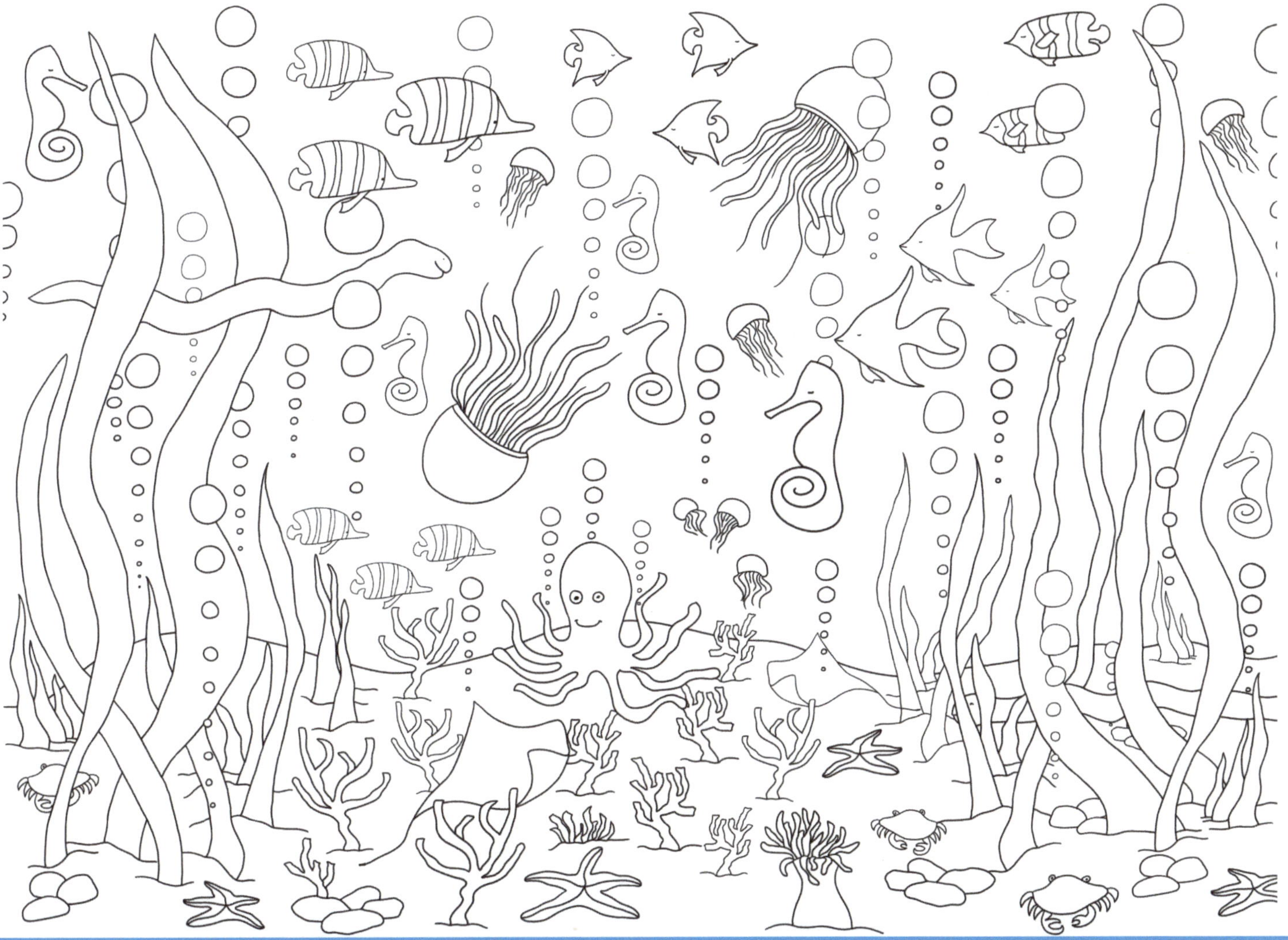

DID YOU KNOW: God knows how many fish swim in the sea and how many birds fly in the air—all of creation is under His command!

At the Finish, God will judge all people.

This means that He will reward those who love and obey Him and punish those who do not.

You can be sure that I live forever.
And you can be just as sure that I will sharpen my flashing sword.
My hand will hold it when I judge.
I will get even with my enemies.
I will pay back those who hate Me.

Deuteronomy 32: 40-41

As God's children, we have the right to make declarations or decrees on His behalf!

Fill in the blanks with the missing words from the song.

WE MAGNIFY YOU Discovery Collection: Workbook 8

We are God's **righteous ones** because we walk in His ways, doing what is right in His eyes.

Let's ask the Holy Spirit to continue to help us to walk faithfully with God, so that our actions and choices will always show God that He is important to us!

Arise, shine, for your light has come, and the glory of the Lord rises upon you.

Isaiah 60:1

Find these words from the song hidden in the puzzle below:

☐ **CREATION** ☐ **AMEN** ☐ **DECREE**

☐ **COMMAND** ☐ **STAND** ☐ **JUDGEMENT**

☐ **RIGHTEOUS** ☐ **KINGDOM**

T	C	O	M	M	A	N	D	S	D	G	A	A	T
T	O	A	R	I	G	H	T	E	O	U	S	S	M
E	E	D	N	K	I	N	G	D	O	M	T	E	T
J	J	A	I	S	E	N	N	N	R	A	I	C	O
A	D	A	N	M	N	E	T	M	N	N	H	R	E
I	R	N	G	N	S	M	T	D	E	M	E	E	A
E	M	D	A	N	E	A	H	S	M	M	N	A	I
N	U	D	E	A	I	M	I	M	S	S	A	T	T
J	G	I	E	N	I	C	N	C	D	G	T	I	S
O	O	R	M	C	T	S	G	G	D	A	I	O	O
D	G	N	N	J	R	E	S	O	A	D	O	N	A
I	I	A	N	T	N	E	A	S	N	N	N	U	S
E	C	O	N	E	O	S	E	U	S	N	S	N	M
H	R	E	N	A	S	T	S	E	O	U	E	G	G

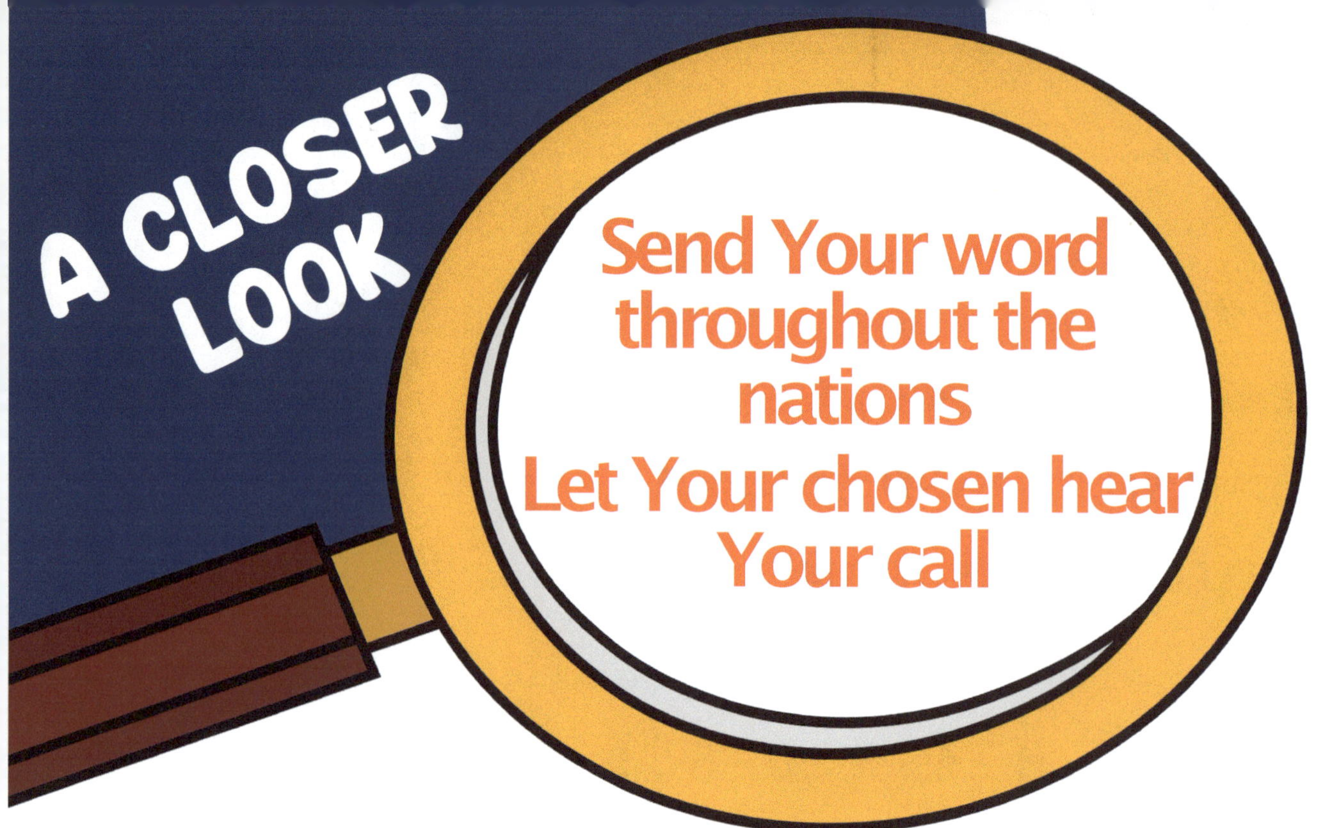

One of the final commands that Jesus gave to His disciples was to go out to the nations and spread the word of the Lord.

We partner with God to:

- Declare His will for the Earth

- Call His chosen people into His Kingdom

- Set an example for all nations to see His Glory, mercy and goodness by the way we live our lives.

Match the scrambled words to
their solution:

EEDREC •	• COMMAND
ONCRAITE •	• NATIONS
MMODANC •	• CHOSEN
NASNIOT •	• PEOPLE
NSDTA •	• GLORY
SHNOEC •	• DECREE
LEPEOP •	• CREATION
LGRYO •	• STAND

WE MAGNIFY YOU Discovery Collection: Workbook 8

Oneness and Holiness are very, very, very, important to God. So, we sing this to let Him know that we need His help to **make us one, His holy people.**

When we dwell together in perfect harmony, together as one, we show the world exactly what God is like – Father, Son and Holy Spirit working together as one.

When the world sees that in us, God's glory is revealed. How amazing! What an incredible job we have to do together - to reveal the Glory of God to the entire earth!

Draw faces and clothes on the people, and color them in to help you remember we are **ONE** as God's people across the globe.

For you are a chosen people. You are royal priests, a holy nation, God's very own possession. As a result, you can show others the goodness of God.

1 Peter 2:9

Take some time to reflect on this song. Here's some space to write down your thoughts.

MY JOURNAL

CPSIA information can be obtained
at www.ICGtesting.com
Printed in the USA
BVHW020556241219
567629BV00015B/244/P